FAITH :

Whose Is It?

FAITH :

Whose Is It?

Jackie Burgus

Destiny Image Publishers
P.O. Box 351
Shippensburg, PA 17257

"Speaking to the Purposes of God for this Generation"

I.S.B.N. 0-914903-55-1

For Worldwide Distribution
Printed in the U.S.A.

Dedication

I wish to thank my family for their continued support and tireless effort in assisting me in the completion of this book. I wish to especially thank our daughters, Lynn and Lori, for critiquing the manuscript and for their invaluable input and objective review of it.

About the Author

Jackie Burgus is an anointed Bible teacher whose wide range of experience in religious teaching has made her a qualified helper for those desiring a deeper walk with the Lord.

As a licensed minister and former chaplain for a variety of women's clubs, Mrs. Burgus has inspired others with her experience and understanding in the areas of prayer, evangelism, intercession and leadership training. In addition, her clarity in teaching the Word of God has been seen in her twenty-five years of experience in leading both children's and adult Bible studies and seminars.

In recent years Mrs. Burgus has been a guest speaker on several television shows, and she has also been the featured speaker at Women's Aglow meetings. Her teaching and ministry have taken her to other countries as well. In addition to authoring this book, she has written a book entitled *God-Given Territory: A Strategy to Keep It!*

Mrs. Burgus, resides in Tulsa, Oklahoma, and is the wife of Dr. Roger Burgus, professor at a local university. They are both active in various Christian organizations. If you would like further information, contact them at P.O. Box 701822, Tulsa, OK 74170.

Contents

Introduction

Many years ago an evangelistic organization distributed a tract which illustrated a deep gulf between man and God. In the next illustration they placed a bridge which man could cross in order to leave the kingdom of darkness (the earthly realm) and enter the Kingdom of God (the heavenly realm). This bridge was Jesus and by believing in Him and asking Him to be our personal Saviour, we could cross that bridge! Once we were in the Kingdom of God we were God's children forever.

Think about the time you made that decision to ask Jesus to be your Saviour and Lord. Think about what you experienced. Do you remember how His presence produced a joy within you and the great welcome the members of the body of Christ gave you? I can see in my mind's eye the great gathering of Christians on God's side of the bridge rejoicing and praising God as each new sister or brother joins them. It's a time of celebration, and all focus their attention on worshipping God.

I wish that my mind's eye could continue to see this and this alone, but soon I begin to see the body of Christ divide into little gatherings here and there. I'm wondering what is causing this to happen. Some of the faces become filled with discouragement while others appear to be confident in their proclamations. My spirit-man begins to experience a grieving which I cannot comprehend. I find myself crying, "Holy Spirit, what is this in the body of Christ? Why do I grieve and weep within?" Then I hear Him speak to my spirit that division is grievous to the Father.

What is grieving the Father's heart? He is grieving over His children's separating and dividing themselves on issues of His gifts. He's grieving that any would require the allegiance of another to their given doctrine. One of the issues has been the various positions taken on faith. A part of Christ's body believe that we are heavily involved (on a personal level) with the gift of faith. They believe this involvement determines our failure or success. Others have been adamant that there should be no expression of this faith because we have little or no involvement; it's solely God's. As a result, many have been wounded, discouraged and deeply hurt by others' attitudes and approaches to this gift. Between the two poles of this issue there lies the unity God desires.

My mind's eye could see this grievous state of the body of Christ because I've been exposed to the effects of these various doctrines on individual children within God's family. I've ministered to dear saints who have been totally crushed by thinking they were at fault for their faith's not working. Other precious ones have taken a totally passive position on the question of faith, and this has allowed Satan to rule them.

Just as Jesus became the bridge for all of us to reach the Father, the Father has a bridge for all of us to be in unity on the issue of faith.

If we can see what He sees and know what He knows, then we can lay aside our doctrines and embrace one another in love and unity. This is my desire in writing this book. May what I share bring light to your understanding, hope to your heart and healing between you and your brethren in the body of Christ. May this work help to bridge the differing views on the function of faith just as Jesus bridged the gap between God and man.

CHAPTER 1

The Source of Faith

PART I

Faith is God's Gift to Man

Have you ever thought, "I wish I had enough faith," or, "I know that if I had enough faith, things would work out," or, "I'm failing God because I don't have enough faith!"?

Did you know that statements like these — whether you think them or someone else questions you with them —are wrong? Let me explain by looking at the truths as reported in the Word of God about faith and your involvement.

First, let's see what the Bible says faith is: "Now faith is the assurance (confirmation, the title deed) of the things (we) hope for, being the proof of things (we) do not see and the conviction of their reality — faith perceiving as real fact what is not revealed to the senses." (AMP)

Now let's read Romans 12:3:

> For through the grace given to me I say to every man among you not to think more highly of himself than he ought to think; but to think so as to have

sound judgment, as God has *allotted* to each a measure of faith. (NAS) (The Amplified Bible says, "...each according to the degree of faith apportioned by God to him.")

To *allot* means to assign or to give a measured portion of something. In our case, God has measured and given a portion of faith to *all men*. Paul is saying in Romans 12:3 that God has assigned a portion of trust and confidence in Himself to all men so they may come to believe in, adhere to, and depend upon Him and what His Word states. So faith is a gift from God to man. I Corinthians 7:17 says, "Let each one seek to conduct himself and regulate his affairs so as to lead the life which the Lord has *allotted* and *imparted* to him." [1] If we are to implement God's principles to activate or release the gift of faith, we'll need to start out with what is most important to God. In this scripture, He's saying our lives are to be controlled by Him, for by His great love and mercy and faithfulness toward us He has planned a life for us that will be abundant in all aspects if we submit ourselves to Him. By His gift of faith, God has placed an assurance in us that we can hope in God and not be disappointed. We can know without a doubt that we have what God has promised without seeing it or touching it!

Martin Luther caught the revelation of this when he meditated on Ephesians 2:8. Paul writes, "For by grace you have been saved through faith; and that not of yourselves, it is the gift of God." It's true Paul is talking about the gift of salvation, but look how that salvation came about. First, salvation came to us by grace (unmerited favor), which is a gift from God and then by faith, which Paul says is a faith that didn't come from our own resources. If this faith didn't come from our own person, it must be a gift from God. So it would be correct to say that in Ephesians 2:8 we find three gifts given to mankind by God: grace, faith, and salvation.

You're probably thinking, "She said that God had measured a portion of faith, so I'm not able to go beyond my portion." Wrong! Any gift given by God to man is always far in excess of man's needs or wants. In Ephesians 3:20 Paul writes, "Now to Him who is *able* to do exceeding abundantly *beyond* all that we ask or think, according to the power that works within us..." Notice that Paul says nothing is beyond God nor is His ability limited!

A good example of God's plenty is His dealing with me in the ministry. In a still small voice He spoke to me and said, "Jackie, anything that happens in the ministry that I've called you to will be supernatural. You won't have anything to do with it." My first thought was, "Boy, what a relief! I'm just to let Him have His way and He will promote me in what He desires." In other words, the power that worketh within me is not mine, but God's, and therein lies exceeding abundance.

So what are we to conclude: that the gift of faith is given by God and that the allotment will always be more than we will ever need, so we really don't lack faith. If we don't lack faith, then why do we feel so often that we do? Our problem lies in our lack of understanding. In other words, our involvement with this gift of faith is linked with our ability to understand God's principles and implement them to see this gift of faith activated. In order for this to occur, we must have the living Word of God infused into our spirits, bringing us the understanding that we need.

The first principle of God which we must understand is that God's nature and character, as portrayed in scripture, indicates that He is no respecter of persons and that His gifts, though measured or allotted, are neither small nor large, lesser or greater, but abundant in all aspects. Therefore, we can be confident that each man's gift of *faith* is all he'll ever need.

To confirm this, let's go to His Word to see what it says regarding faith. As I studied the scriptures for God's expressed will on this matter I reached the conclusion that what I stated in the previous paragraph is true. John 3:16 says that God so loved the world that He gave His only begotten Son and that whosoever believed should not perish. To believe takes faith, and according to Paul (who was inspired by the Holy Spirit in his writings), men have the faith to believe, but they simply suppress it and stay in an unrighteous state. So even though Jesus spoke several times about man's inability to come to know Him (Jesus) except the Father draw him and said that He (Jesus) had souls assigned to Him by the Father, we see the scope of how many souls the Father wanted to be saved, in spite of their lack of understanding. Let's read Romans 1:16-20:

> For I am not ashamed of the gospel, for it is the power of God for salvation to every one who believes, to the Jew first and also to the Greek.

For in it the righteousness of God is revealed from faith to faith; as it is written, "BUT THE RIGHTEOUS MAN SHALL LIVE BY FAITH." For the wrath of God is revealed from heaven against all ungodliness and unrighteousness of men, who *suppress* the truth in unrighteousness, because that which is known about God is evident within them [that gift of faith given every man]; for God made it evident to them. For since the creation of the world His invisible attributes, His eternal power and nature, have been clearly seen, being understood through what has been made, so that they are without excuse.

Paul emphasizes that God has created man with the ability to receive His free gift of faith and an ability to see the truth when it is presented. Why then do men suppress the truth? Realize that not all who suppress the "truth" desire to do evil. Many times good people will draw the wrong conclusion about who God is based on circumstances, tragedies, or the unchristian actions of others who profess to be Christians. They decide that if *God were God* He would prevent these tragedies, circumstances, etc. This would be what we should expect if God had made man a robot, programming him to do His will. The opposite of this is true, for God gave each person a free will. Each is given an opportunity to respond to His love and to decide to do His will rather than his own will. Man is also influenced by another spiritual force (the devil and his hosts), which is opposed to the goodness of God made evident. The devil seeks to inspire men to murder, to destroy, to hate and to make war against one another.

A good example of God's goodness made evident would be His efforts to warn the Jewish people in Europe of Satan's murderous plan to destroy them. Some thirty years before the actual master plan of extermination was implemented by Hitler, God spoke to the Jewish people across Europe to flee, for destruction was coming. He spoke through their Rabbis, through members of the Jewish community, and through small flare-ups of oppressive acts against them. God willed to save them, but because they were free to choose, they chose to stay and live in their present prosperity and suppress the truth God was speaking to them. God was giving them an opportunity to experience His abundant provision for them by putting their trust in Him and leaving all they could see for the place of safety He'd already assigned them. If they had understood it was His power that was working within them through their allotted measure of faith, they would have been saved from the enemy's destruction.

The wrong conclusions drawn by us or others can be eliminated when we understand that *all* have the gift of faith, and activating it depends upon our accepting this gift of faith as ours and allowing the Holy Spirit to be a part of our lives. As we allow this power of God's to work within us, we will see His will, purpose and provision manifested in our lives. It is also necessary for us to understand that this gift of faith is abundant, but it will be activated in stages, based on our ability to release ourselves into the Holy

Spirit's power: hearing a specific word for us, trusting that what we've heard is from God, depending upon God to bring it to pass, resting in the knowledge that it's His work, and yielding all of the care of its fulfillment over to Him. It is reassuring to know that as our needs surface, God will activate our faith by His supernatural power through the Holy Spirit and that we become participants of faith as we cooperate with what the Father is doing.

A WORD OF CAUTION! Be watchful that you don't compare the activation of your faith with that of another. Your faith's activation may appear to be greater or lesser than another, but that is not your concern. It is the job of the Holy Spirit to activate what each of us needs when we need it. What is our job? The disciples knew they had one and asked Jesus what it was. Jesus said, "This is the work you do, believe in Me and He who sent Me."

Let's observe a child in his relationship to God. He's so simple in his approach, he has no trouble believing God for what he has asked. When Jesus said "Suffer the little children to come unto Me," I'm sure He answered their requests and that they, as a matter of fact, believed Him and received.

When our children were smaller, each one of the girls had a cat. One day Lori came home with a small kitten which she had found locked in a locker at school. Someone had cut all its whiskers off, but other than that he was a very healthy kitten. I was not pleased to have another cat in the house, but when Jeff saw the kitten he exclaimed, "Praise the Lord! I asked God for a gray tiger like you always wanted, Momma, and I asked if I could have a cat of my very own like Lynn and Lori. Praise the Lord! He gave me both!" Well now, I couldn't argue with God about His answer, could I? Jeff's childlike faith had given him a cat, and truly I had always wanted a gray tiger. Jeff never thought to question his faith in God. He never wondered if he was given faith; he just accepted what was allotted him.

Let's study faith in the natural also. When a child asks his parents to go to the zoo, and the parents say "yes," the child is satisfied that they'll be going. Having heard the response to his request, he goes on to the next question: "When will we go to the zoo?" The parents say, "On Saturday." Now the child is satisfied. Between the time he asked and Saturday, he may come and ask if it's time, but he'll never question whether they'll really be going. In other words, he doesn't work at believing his parents' words to him.

The child took his parents' word and that is what God wants us to do: take Him at His word. There is something very endearing to us as adults when we see a child trusting us or others. In like fashion, we delight our heavenly Father when we accept His gift of faith allotted to us.

Just as the child had questions about the trip planned for the zoo, we will have questions about the who, what, why and when of faith. All these questions are normal, but we need not question whether or not we have faith.

PART II

The Purpose of the Gift of Faith

Since we all have *all* the faith we will ever need, what does God want to produce in our lives through this faith? Here is a list of some of the areas the Father desires to see fulfilled in our lives:

1. A good work in us.
Philippians 1:6 — Paul says he's confident that the work God has begun is good.

2. A perfection in us.
Psalms 138:8 (KJV) states that He will perfect that which concerneth us.

3. A trust in Him.
Hebrews 10:23 tells us we can hold fast to our confession without wavering, for our God is faithful.

4. The knowledge that He'll preserve us for the day of Jesus Christ.
I Thessalonians 5:23 assures us that God Himself sanctifies us and preserves us completely until our Lord's return.

5. His enrichment of us.
I Corinthians 1:4 emphasizes that in everything we are enriched by Christ Jesus.

6. A testimony that we belong to Him.
I Corinthians 1:8 says that we will be found blameless and that God will confirm us to the end.

7. A release of His gifts in us.
I Corinthians 4:7 tells us that even as the Father has confirmed us, He also gives us all His gifts. "...you are not lacking in any gift."

8. An ability to fellowship with His Son.
I Corinthians 1:9 reveals that we were called unto fellowship with His Son, Jesus Christ our Lord.

9. An everlasting peace.
Romans 5:1 tells us our faith justifies us, and therefore we have peace with God through our Lord, Jesus Christ.

10. A sense of protection from the enemy.
II Thessalonians 3:3 confirms that God will strengthen and protect us.

11. A confidence of the destiny He's planned for us.
I Thessalonians 5:9 promises that God has destined us for salvation through our Lord Jesus Christ.

12. A sure foundation — we live together with Him.
I Thessalonians 5:10 lays a sure foundation by Christ's death, which ushers us into a life together with God now and forever.

As we read the scriptures concerning God's attitude toward us and His desire to keep us, protect us and perfect us through this gift of faith, we again come to understand God's design to bring us to perfection. To perfect means to lack nothing which is essential. To lack nothing which is essential, in our case, starts first with the fact that *faith* given by God is lacking in nothing essential to our existence.

Our perfection is based not on our ability, but on God's faithfulness to work His abilities and character in us. We have, at our new birth and salvation, through confession of Jesus Christ as Lord, been transformed into God's image in our spirit man. But God wants us to know that the same gift of faith which brought that miracle is with us to continue transforming our minds and bodies into the image of God.

All that we need in the perfection (lacking in nothing essential) is already housed within us, for the fulness of the Deity dwells with our spirit — man awaiting the time when we will allow the release of God's strength, God's character, God's hope, God's endurance, God's peace, God's joy, God's harmony and God's armor (Colossians 2:9).

Paul says in Romans 5:12 that the same faith that has justified us also brings us grace which enables us to stand and to hope. As we read on in chapter six of Romans, Paul explains in great detail the nature of this grace which we've received by faith:

> Therefore we have been buried with Him through baptism into death, in order that as Christ was raised

from the dead through the glory of the Father, so we too might walk in newness of life.

For if we have become united with Him in the likeness of His death, certainly we shall be also in the likeness of His resurrection, knowing this, that our old self was crucified with Him, that our body of sin might be done away with, that we should no longer be slaves to sin; for he who has died is freed from sin.

Now if we have died with Christ, we believe that we shall also live with Him, knowing that Christ, having been raised from the dead, is never to die again; death no longer is master over Him.

For the death that He died, He died to sin, once for all; but the life that He lives, He lives to God.

Even so consider yourselves to be dead to sin, but alive to God in Christ Jesus.

Therefore do not let sin reign in your mortal body that you should obey its lust, and do not go on presenting the members of your body to sin as instruments of unrighteousness; but present yourselves to God as those alive from the dead, and your members as instruments of righteousness to God.

For sin shall not be master over you, for you are not under law, but under grace. (Romans 6:4-14 NAS)

Paul says we are destined for newness of life because of our transformation from Satan's kingdom into God's kingdom.

I think all of us would say at one time or another, "I'd like to start over," or, "I'd like a new life," or, "I'd like to erase the past." The good news of the Gospel of Jesus Christ is that we do start a new life with Him. This new life is so new that each day it is possible to start over again. Let me explain: Many times we, as Christians, find ourselves in a place we know we should not be in our relationship with God. In order to return to where we need to be, we must repent and ask God to start a new life in us again. This new life I'm talking about is in the area of our minds and bodies. We are assured that the gift of faith which brings the grace to live the new life is ours:

Much more then, having been justified by His blood, we shall be saved from the wrath of God through Him. (Romans 5:9)

God has purposely justified us, given us faith in Himself, and given us the grace (ability) to live our lives through Him so that we will find it easy to release more and more of ourselves to His control. God is not interested in controlling us for power or self-gain. He already has all power, but He is such a loving God that He wants to perfect that which concerns us for our sakes. He wants us to lack nothing essential to our existence. However, He can do this only by our submission to Him so that His gifts of faith, grace and justification can be manifested.

For God has not destined us for wrath, but for obtaining salvation through our Lord Jesus Christ, who died for us, that whether we are awake or asleep. We many live together with Him.

Now may the God of peace Himself sanctify you entirely; and may your spirit and soul and body be preserved complete. Without blame at the coming of our Lord Jesus Christ (I Thessalonians 5:9-10; 23-24, NAS).

Verse 23 says that the God of peace *Himself* sanctifies you *entirely*. Being entirely sanctified is being perfected. Paul continues to declare that our spirit, soul and body can be made complete without blame. Paul follows this statement by telling how it can happen: "Faithful is He who calls you, and He also will bring it to pass."

When we realize that God the Father has, through Jesus Christ and the Holy Spirit, already given us everything that is essential and that He vowed to bring this perfection to pass in our lives, we'll desire to let Him bring it to pass. It is truly amazing to me that the God of the Universe would bring everything to us and that we can accept or reject Him and His gifts. But this I do believe: people will say, "Yes, Lord," if they realize it's already been done for them. Faith is theirs; grace is theirs; salvation is theirs; newness of life in the spirit, soul and body is theirs just for the asking.

When we ask as people of God, we are positioned in the flow of His faithfulness. God Himself elected us to this position as His sons and daughters. He elected to meet all conditions for us. What a loving Father He is!

CHAPTER II

Activating Your Faith

God desires for us to have a working trust, an active rest in Him and in what He said or says. Our faith walk should not be a struggle; it should be an opening up of one dimension after another of understanding the *total reliability* of God, an understanding of His ability to take care of us. Our struggles will cease when we understand that God truly wants to meet our every need and that His timing to do so is perfect. God's dependability activates the gift of faith that He has already put within us. As we enter into this trust and rest He is then able to show us more and more of Himself, in turn activating this gift of faith in a greater measure than before. We need this faith to be activated so that we can see into the infinite where God lives, for we are creatures living in the finite. You see, God is infinite and His gifts reflect Him. This gift of faith is more than we will ever touch in our finite time on earth. That is why Paul says it is exceedingly abundantly above all we ask or think. This gift of faith will carry us on into eternity (or into infinity) with God.

We cannot cause the release of this gift of faith, but God, in His great mercy and loving kindness toward us, causes our faith to expand. We do have a part to play: to allow God to do it by submitting our wills to Him. When He speaks something to our hearts, we must say "yes" to Him and trust Him to bring into manifestation everything which He has spoken.

How do we say "yes" to God? There are certain principles revealed to us through the scriptures for us to follow. Then God is able to activate our gift of faith within us.

PRINCIPLE NUMBER ONE: COMMUNION WITH GOD

We are to be in communion with God continually. Through the power of the Holy Spirit, we are able to pray as we ought (Romans 8:26). As we continue in our time with Him, this will cause us to say, "Yes, Lord," and this will be the releasing factor of our faith. What we will see by our communion with the Lord will be the all-sufficiency of the gift of faith already housed within us. (If you have problems hearing the voice of the Holy Spirit in your communion time, under "Interpreting the Voice of the Holy Spirit," chapter five would be helpful to you.)

By this constant communion with God, we'll stop working to get more faith and realize it's already in us. We'll realize that because we've said "yes" to our Lord Jesus Christ, we're not responsible for our responsibilities. He is. Let me explain: "Lord" means master or ruler. When we make a decision to let Jesus Christ be our Lord, we give everything to Him, including our responsibilities. By practicing this first principle in our lives we can experience this freedom: "Jesus therefore was saying to those Jews who had believed Him, 'If you abide in My word, then you are truly disciples of Mine; and you shall know the truth, and the truth shall make you free.'" (John 8:32, NAS)

Combining the work of the Holy Spirit with the freedom Jesus promised, we are able to enter into the throne room of God. This affords us the way to commune with God.

Hebrews 10:19-24 says:

Since therefore, brethren, we have confidence to enter the holy place by the blood of Jesus, by a new and living way which He inaugurated for us through the veil, that is, His flesh, and since we have a great priest over the house of God, let us draw near with a sincere heart in full assurance of faith, having our hearts sprinkled clean from an evil conscience and our bodies washed with pure water.

Let us hold fast the confession of our hope without wavering, for He who promised is faithful.

In these passages we see the wonder of what Jesus did for us. He freed us of sin and made us holy in the sight of God. Through our Lord's sacrifice we are able to have intimate communion with the Father in His throne room.

In the following scripture, notice that Jesus is interceding for us in order that the work of the Holy Spirit might be done in us. Hebrews 7:25:

Hence, also, He is able to save forever those who

draw near to God through Him, since He always lives to make intercession for them.

And finally Hebrews 4:14-16:

Since then we have a great high priest who has passed through the heavens, Jesus the Son of God, let us hold fast our confession,

For we do not have a high priest who cannot sympathize with our weakness, but one who has been tempted in all things as we are, yet without sin.

Let us therefore draw near with confidence to the throne of grace, that we may receive mercy and may find grace to help in time of need.

We would not have been told that we had access to the throne room of God unless it were possible to experience being in His presence. This throne room time with God is the most precious thing possible. It allows us to understand what's on the heart of the Father, and it allows Him to reveal our hearts to us for encouragement and correction. What a true joy it is to discover, in our communion time with Him, that God is working His desires in us so that we may come into harmony with our Maker's plans!

Many think that it is a difficult thing to come into the throne room of God, but it's not. The blood of Jesus has torn the veil which at one time separated us from God, and now we can step into His throne room as easily as we walk through a natural doorway.

When I go to God's throne room I don't wonder if I'll

get in; I know I will. If sin is found in my members, the Holy Spirit brings that to my attention, and we deal with it.

When I am with Him in His throne room, somehow, in His own way, He orchestrates bringing me into praise and worship, cleansing me and restoring fellowship. This is because I'm covered by the blood of Jesus. Truly there is nothing like it in our visible world. Nothing is more satisfying or beautiful for us to experience!

PRINCIPLE NUMBER TWO: FAITH COMETH BY HEARING

Romans 10:17 says faith comes by hearing and hearing by the Word of God. Romans 10:17 is really saying your gift of faith is activated by hearing God's Word. The Word of God is alive and sharper than any two-edged sword (Hebrews 12:4). Faith is released or activated by hearing and reading the Word of God. Faith is expanded by our experience with God.

To gain a greater understanding of what I'm saying, let's use an example of natural (earthly) faith. When a child is born, he trusts everyone to take care of him. That's faith in others. If he is in a good situation with responsible, loving, caring adults, that trust or faith will continue to expand as he is exposed to more and more caring acts from the adults around him. If the reverse is true, then his natural faith or trust in others will be diminished, and his perspective of life and living will be affected. It will cause a shutting-down or a deactivation of this trust in others. In supernatural faith, we are born into a good environment.

To experience an expansion of faith as God intended, we must continually be exposed to the Word of God. In this way, the Holy Spirit is able to make the Word of God alive or active in our lives. We come to experience His trustworthiness, and we know without a doubt that we can lean upon, depend on, rely upon and be confident in Him and in His supernatural power, which is released on our behalf.

As you can see, supernatural faith, as manifested in our spiritual lives, is quite different from natural faith, for God has imparted His supernatural realm to all, equally. In the case of natural faith, not everyone can be assured of an opportunity to have his trust in others developed or expanded.

PRINCIPLE NUMBER THREE: MEDITATING ON HIS WORD

Meditating on the Word of God is the next principle to be applied. Meditating is different from simply reading or hearing it. Many times we can look at certain situations and be so overwhelmed by them that our initial reaction is to think that there is no way that God can do anything. Or we may think, "God, I'm sorry, but I can't trust You to help in this: there are just too many things to consider!" In times like these, meditating can bring us back to the expansion of our gift of faith. Joshua 1:8-9 says,

> This book of the law shall not depart from your mouth, but you shall meditate on it day and night, so that you may be careful to do according to all that is written in it; for then you will make your way

prosperous, and then you will have success. Have I not commanded you? Be strong and courageous! Do not tremble or be dismayed, for the Lord your God is with you wherever you go.

Several years ago, I was meditating on a number of scripture passages. I'd been reading them several times a day for well over a month when suddenly, I saw a connection between two of the passages that electrified my spirit and my mind.

Ephesians 3:16-19:

...that He would grant you, according to the riches of His glory, to be strengthened with power through His Spirit in the inner man; so that Christ may dwell in your hearts through faith; and that you, being rooted and grounded in love, may be able to *comprehend* with all the saints what is the breadth and length and height and depth, and to know the love of Christ which surpasses knowledge, that you may be filled up to all the fulness of God.

Romans 8:35-39:

Who shall separate us from the love of Christ? Shall tribulation, or distress, or persecution, or famine, or nakedness, or peril, or sword?

Just as it is written, 'For Thy sake we are being put to death all day long; we were considered as sheep to be slaughtered.'

But in all these things we overwhelmingly conquer through Him who loved us.

For I am convinced that neither death, nor life, nor angels, nor principalities, nor things present, nor things to come, nor powers, nor height, nor depth, nor any other created thing, shall be able to separate us from the love of God, which is in Christ Jesus our Lord.

I saw that the connecting link between them was *to comprehend*. Paul comprehended something, he related in Ephesians 3, that gave him an absolute assurance of God's love so he could write Romans 8:35-39. What electrified my whole being was that Paul comprehended the scope of the love of God. So much so, that he could write Romans 8:35-39 in full assurance that literally nothing could separate us from God and His love for us. Paul knew that perfect love casts out fear. To be perfect is lacking in no essential detail, to be complete or absolute. Paul had comprehended the essential details of the dimensions of God's love toward those who believe. This is why Paul could write in absolute assurance that no height was greater than God's height, no depth was greater than God's depth, no length was greater than God's length, and no width was greater than God's width. Paul says, "...nor any other created thing, shall be able to separate us from the love of God, which is in Christ Jesus our Lord." All the adversities Paul was describing could only be caused by created things (man or spirits) and they are nothing compared with God's love and its power!

What electrified me about all this? I realized that because I was a fellow heir with Paul, I could experience what Paul had came to know of the love of God. Paul was speaking from a voice of experience when he listed all the adversities that could befall us as Christians.

Paul knew that we, as Christians, would desperately need this revelation in order to stand in the battle and to keep our faith active in our relationship to God. In case no one has told you, we are at war and the enemy doesn't cease fire — ever!

I'm so grateful for the Holy Spirit's power working this revelation in me. I know that if I am not committed to meditating on the Word of God, the Holy Spirit cannot bring vital information to me, and my faith could be deactivated by adversities.

If we fail to follow this principle of meditating on the Word of God, we cause our gift of faith to lie dormant. Just as a tree remains dormant in the winter, so it is with our faith, if we do not meditate on God's Word. There is life in the tree, but it's not active. The gift of faith is in us, but it will not be active if we fail to follow God's principles.

Meditation takes us from hoping in God and His Word to having an absolute assurance that He is causing things to happen that we cannot see with our natural eyes, but which we fully expect to be made manifest in the natural at the right time — His time.

To meditate successfully, you must dictate to your mind what you will allow it to think. How do you do this? You have power over your mind when you speak to it in the name of Jesus, for He has authority over all things. You must not allow your mind to meditate on things that are contrary to the Word of God. Your spirit and your mind need to be united as one concerning the Word of God or you will be doubleminded and unproductive (James 1:6-8). To have your mind and spirit man united in purpose and thought is the only way you can consistently do all that is written in God's Word so that you may prosper in all your ways (Joshua 1:8).

By applying the principles of hearing and meditating, you are allowing God to activate the gift of faith within you. If you won't allow these principles to operate in you, then circumstances, people, etc. will sway you, and that will shut down active faith. By meditating on the Word of God, you can be built up, and your perspective will be from God's viewpoint, not your own.

PRINCIPLE NUMBER FOUR: STAY HIDDEN IN CHRIST

We are to remain *hidden* in Christ, for in Him is dwelling the fulness of God. Colossians 2:9-10 says:

> For in Him all the fulness of Deity dwells in bodily form and in Him you have been made complete (perfect, absolute, lacking nothing essential), and He is the head over all rule and authority; (NAS)

Reading on in the book of Colossians, we find in chapter 3:1-3:

> If then you have been raised up with Christ, keep seeking the things above, where Christ is, seated at the right hand of God.

Set your mind on the things above, not on the things that are on earth.

For you have died and your life is hidden with Christ in God. (NAS)

The fulness of the Deity is indwelling every Christian. This fulness includes His character and nature. To be hidden in Christ is to be covered or concealed. As we read on in the third chapter of Colossians we will find out why the covering or concealment is so important. As we are hidden in Christ, and our eyes are focused on Him, we are covered so that the enemies of our beings, the enemies of our faith in God, will not overtake us. Paul lists in detail the things which can be avoided by staying hidden in Christ: immorality, impurity, passion, evil desires, greed (which amounts to idolatry) need not be found among us. Remaining hidden in Christ frees us from anger, wrath, malice, slander and abusive speech from our mouths. Paul's confidence in our ability to be free of these idolatries was based on the fact that Jesus Christ is all in all, and through Him, we've been made complete.

In all aspects of our new life in Christ, we must choose to walk in the revelation given to us. So it is with this principle of being dead and hidden in Christ. I could write a volume on the book of Colossians, but instead, I want to encourage you to meditate upon it for yourself. One attribute of God I do wish to point out is the love of God. If you desire to have your gift of faith come into the fulness that God intended, you must let your new nature (God's nature) have its way in you. This means starting with the greatest attribute of God, His love.

PRINCIPLE NUMBER FIVE:
LOVE WITH HIS LOVE

And so, as those who have been chosen of God, holy and beloved, put on a heart of compassion, kindness, humility, gentleness and patience. Bearing with one another, and forgiving each other, whoever has a complaint against any one, just as the Lord forgave you, so also should you.

And beyond all these things put on love, which is the perfect bond of unity. (Colossians 3:12-14, NAS)

Earlier I said it was necessary for us to say "yes" to God if He is going to activate our faith. This is certainly true in loving with God's kind of love. James says faith without works is dead and *where there is no love neither active faith nor God-inspired works will happen.* It is very important for us, as Christians, to yield ourselves to the Holy Spirit and allow Him to cause the love of God to flow through us. By an act of our will we can say, "Father, in the name of Jesus, as an act of my will, I give You permission to have Your love flow through me to others." Our own revelation of the dynamics of God's love will bring us to the same place that Paul came to in his writings on the subject of God's love. Paul said that it would never fade out or become obsolete, that it would never come to an end and that nothing could separate us from the love of God. If the precious gift of faith is to blossom in us as planned, we must have God's love flowing freely through us to others.

PRINCIPLE NUMBER SIX: FORGIVENESS OF OTHERS

Forgiveness of others goes hand in glove with love.

For if you forgive men for their transgressions, your heavenly Father will also forgive you. But if you do not forgive men, then your Father will not forgive your transgressions. (Matthew 6:14-15, NAS).

In Matthew 6:14-15, Jesus wanted all who were listening to understand this principle. It is not that God our Father does not want to forgive, but He can't forgive known sin that has not been confessed. Any time we are in unforgiveness toward another, we are in sin. Any time we are in sin, our communion with the Lord suffers greatly, and we find it hard to know or do His will. All our activities as Christians are affected. We've broken our fellowship with God, which is His power plant to activate our faith. How do we forgive when we don't feel like it? We forgive the same way we love, by an act of our will. We permit God's forgiveness to flow through to the one who has offended us. We want to keep the channels clear in our relationship with God. Staying in unforgiveness has a price tag too high for any Christian! We'll share more on this later, for the enemy has his way of using unforgiveness against us.

PRINCIPLE NUMBER SEVEN: FELLOWSHIP OF THE BODY

Fellowship with the body of Christ is a must! The last two principles and this one are summed up in the following scripture:

And have put on the new man, which is renewed in knowledge after the image of him that created him: where there is neither Greek nor Jew, circumcision nor uncircumcision, Barbarian, Scythian, bond nor free: but Christ is all, and in all. Put on therefore, as the elect of God, holy and beloved, bowels of mercies, kindness, humbleness of mind, meekness, longsuffering; forbearing one another, and forgiving one another, if any man have quarrel against any: even as Christ forgave you, so also do ye. And above all these things put on charity [love], which is the bond of perfectness. And let the peace of God rule in your hearts, to which also ye are called in one body; and be ye thankful. Let the word of Christ dwell in you richly in all wisdom; teaching and admonishing one another in psalms and hymns and spiritual songs, singing with grace in your hearts to the Lord. (Colossians 3:10-16, KJV)

The purposes outlined by Paul for us in Colossians are fulfilled by following the instructions in this same portion of scripture. Paul says as the body of Christ, we need each other in order to learn to dwell richly in love, forbearance, forgiveness, wisdom, teaching and correction. When we follow this admonition, we gather together, and we encourage one another by our testimony of God's faithfulness to us. Paul says we also learn to forbear and forgive through fellowship with the brethren. All of us have experienced a release of our faith as the presence of the

Holy Spirit falls upon us while psalms or spiritual songs or hymns are being sung. We've experienced the release of our faith as we are sharing a burden with others. As they pray for us, we experience God's touch. Through this ministry of the body of Christ to us, we know His peace and His presence.

Are you wondering if God will do for you in your situation what He's done for others? A resounding "Yes!". Fellowship with His Bride, the church, and see Him do His works in you. Remember, "Faithful is He who calls you, and He also will bring it to pass (I Thessalonians 5:24, NAS).

CHAPTER III

Deactivating Our Faith

PART I

Stumbling Blocks to Faith

VISIBILITY ZERO: CALLING CONTROL CENTER!

If the spiritual atmosphere were exclusively God's and ours, we would not have a need for this chapter. The truth is that just as God is desiring to expand our faith and trust in Him, Satan is busy trying to destroy our confidence in God and His Word. We make a moment by moment decision whom we listen to and whom we side with. In order to avoid stumbling in our faith walk, let's look at what will cause our faith and trust in God to be diminished.

One of the first tactics of the enemy is to bring circumstances into our life that appear to be so overwhelming that we are convinced there is no way out! The father of lies would have us believe that our God is incapable of carrying us through these circumstances. How do we combat such an attack? To avoid falling into this trap, don't look at the circumstances with your natural eyes. I know it's easy for me to write, "Don't look at the circumstances," when I'm not walking in your shoes. It's true I don't know your circumstances. I can tell you, however, we do have ways and means to lift our eyes to the heavens from whence cometh our help! If you're in circumstances too monstrous to endure, go to the book of Psalms.

David experienced a vast array of circumstances, many of them monstrous, but he found the key to overcoming them. Let's look at one of David's life experiences to see what I'm talking about. Most of us are familiar with David's encounter with the Philistine giant, Goliath. The Philistines had the armies of Israel held at bay and full of terror. David came to bring provisions to his brothers and discovered the army's situation. David knew it would be necessary for him to kill this giant in order for Israel to win. How could a shepherd boy do something that the armies of Israel were powerless to do? How could he, as one small lad, have the confidence to offer to kill Goliath? David had the confidence to do this because this was not the first time he had trusted God to make him victorious. David, as a shepherd, had killed both a lion and a bear to protect his sheep. This he had done with the help of God. David proclaimed, "Who is this uncircumcised Philistine, (Goliath) that he should taunt (defy) the armies of the living God?" .... Then David said to the Philistine, "You come to me with a sword, a spear and a javelin, but I come to you in the name of the Lord of hosts, the God of the armies of Israel, whom you have taunted" (I Samuel 17:26; 45, NAS). David's proclamation was the affirmation of his complete confidence in God's ability. The difference between David and the armies of Israel, the key which gave him the victory, was that David did not look at the circumstances. David remembered the faithfulness of God in the past. Look at his statement: he calls his God "living." In other words, David was saying, "Goliath, my God is actively working in my life and my circumstances, so I have confidence that He'll deliver you into my hands."

Though I have not experienced anything as life-threatening as a giant, I've known the flow of God's faithfulness toward me and His deliverance from circumstances. This has caused me to draw closer to Him and trust the Father more.

Several years ago, I was placed in the position of choosing among four people, all of whom I loved deeply. Within the span of a few days, my precious father-in-law died, our oldest daughter was in an automobile accident and the doctors found a tumor on the eyelid of our small granddaughter. I wanted to be with all of my family members, but obviously I could not. I went to the Lord and said, "Father, my husband is with Mom Burgus, so which daughter should I go and be with?"

The Holy Spirit spoke to me, "Go be with your mother-in-law." I couldn't believe it!

I said, "Father, my husband is with her. Don't you think I should be with one of our girls?" The same thought came again. So I said, "Father, we're talking about my daughters!"

Then He spoke this: "Whose daughters?"

"Oh," I said, "Lord forgive me, they are Yours, of course."

Then He spoke to my heart again, "Tell me, Jackie, who

is better able to care for them, you or Me?"

I said, "Oh, Father, You by far! I leave them in Your care, and I'll do as You've asked."

When I arrived at the home of my mother-in-law, I found two very tired people. Mom and Roger needed to rest and let someone else answer the phone and fix the meals.

Once I had obeyed, I saw first-hand the faithfulness and power of God on the behalf of *His* daughters. The daughter who had been involved in the accident was removed from intensive care and sent home. The tumor on our grand-daughter's eyelid was benign, and all was well.

Satan might have intended to use this to overwhelm us as a family, but God used it as an opportunity to declare Himself mighty in our midst. God wanted to take our struggles and trials and use them as building blocks to produce fiber, character and proper attitudes, all of which strengthened us rather than causing us to be weakened by the circumstances.

I encourage you to meditate upon the Psalms, and you'll find that you're able to turn your eyes upward to heaven for help, even in the midst of troubles. Go to the Father and say, "Father, you see my circumstances. Now please show me what You see so I can see Your solution. Just as You brought David out of the depths of despair, I know You will bring me out." Look at Psalm 25:14-18; 20-22 (NAS).

> The secret of the Lord is for those who fear Him,
> And He will make them know His covenant.
> My eyes are continually toward the Lord,

Turn to me and be gracious to me,
For He will pluck my feet out of the net.
For I am lonely and afflicted.
    The troubles of my heart are enlarged;
Bring me out of my distresses.
    Look upon my affliction and my trouble,
And forgive all my sins.

    Guard my soul and deliver me;
Do not let me be ashamed, for I take refuge in Thee.
    Let integrity and uprightness preserve me,
For I wait for Thee.
    Redeem Israel, O God,
Out of all his troubles.

The following illustration might help you to understand how we can trust God and His power over our own abilities when circumstances overwhelm us. Circumstances, to us, are somewhat like a cloudy atmosphere is to a pilot. If the pilot is to overcome his circumstances (clouds) so that he can fly, he'll have to rely upon his instruments and the person manning the control center. If he doesn't rely upon his instruments and the instructions from the control center, the plane cannot be flown with safety, and it will crash. Just as it will not help the pilot to look outside while flying in clouds, it will not help us to look to the circumstances surrounding us. Like the pilot who looks only to his instruments and listens only to the voice of the control center, we must look only to the Word of God and listen only to the voice of the Holy Spirit in order to be carried through our circumstances safely.

EMOTIONS: WHO CONTROLS THEM?

Satan's second front is to send hurts into our lives —sometimes through the ones we love the most. Hurts are designed to attack our emotions. Why our emotions? Because our emotions, if not put under the Lordship of Jesus Christ and our spirit-man's control, can do great damage to us and to others. Unchecked emotions cause people to blame God for the Devil's handiwork. Unchecked emotions can establish a permanent wall between people and sometimes, in extreme cases, unchecked emotions can cause people to kill others (e.g. Cain murdered his brother Abel because of jealousy).

Another example of emotions ruling over the Spirit's control would be the case of Peter's emotions. Jesus asked, "Who do you say that I am?" and Peter answered by the Spirit that Jesus was "the Son of God." Jesus then shared about His coming death. Peter could not stand the thought of this happening. Peter loved Jesus so much he let his emotions rule over what the Spirit was saying. Instead of seeking understanding of Jesus' statement about His own death, Peter concerned himself with what he'd feel if Jesus would die. Peter spoke the thoughts Satan had planted within him, "Be it far from thee, Lord: this shall not be unto thee" (KJV). Jesus' seemingly harsh response was not directed at Peter, but to the one who had inspired Peter to speak unbelief. Jesus took this same man and used him mightily for the establishment of His church. Jesus knew that after Peter had experienced the destructiveness of his own emotions the *true* Peter would come forth. Jesus knew that Satan wanted to destroy Peter through his emotions, but He also knew Peter would repent and be filled with a power greater than his emotions. The true Peter would speak before the multitudes. Peter's faith was released to a greater and greater degree as he walked with God in the power of the Holy Spirit. He had learned his lessons well and remained steadfast in faith to the end.

Sometimes we are required to allow the Holy Spirit's control to keep us safe from others' hurts. I recall a situation in our daughter Lori's life as a girl of thirteen. It seems that someone started a rumor about a young man that was very unkind and they gave Lori the credit for the rumor. In his hurt and anger, he vowed to beat her up when he saw her.

It was customary for Lori to walk from her school on Wednesday afternoons to our church for Bible instruction. As Lori was walking to church one day, she saw this young man coming in her direction. She knew that he had seen her and it would not do any good to run, so she cried out to the Lord for help. She knew she was at the mercy of this young man's anger. Just then a large dog came running across the street. The dog circled Lori continually barking at the young man. Because of this, the young man didn't try to harm Lori. As soon as the young man was a good distance away, the owner of the dog came running across the street to get her dog. She explained to Lori how unusual this behavior was for her dog. He had never left the yard before. God had sent the dog on His mission to save Lori! No circumstance is greater than our God.

If you've been hurt emotionally by the action or the inaction of others, God has a way to bring restoration. First, by an act of your will, choose to forgive others; then ask God to work this forgiveness in you. You can also ask God to heal you of those wounds by the healing power of Jesus Christ through the Holy Spirit.

Many times we feel so isolated when we've been wounded in this way and the enemy uses this to his advantage. If you find it difficult to be with others, you may be building walls of protection from further hurts. Realize, dear Saint, you are not alone; many have experienced similar hurts. Look to the Bible to verify what I'm saying.[2] Study the ways people were restored. Seek out others to pray with you.

ATTITUDES MAKE US OR BREAK US

The third way the enemy will try to deactivate your gift of faith is by convincing you that your real problems are caused by other people. When Jesus spoke, "Get thee behind me, Satan," He wasn't speaking to Peter. Jesus wasn't attacking Peter. He was speaking directly to the spirit involved. It would have been an easy thing for Jesus to attack Peter, for Peter had allowed Satan to speak through him. It's much easier to attack an individual who is being used by Satan than to look beyond and see the true source of destruction. This is because we can see the person in living color while Satan must be discerned. Why is it so damaging to our faith to attack people instead of our enemy? Because by doing this, we are entertaining and agreeing with the enemy's thoughts by speaking them out against another person, instead of rebuking the enemy. In doing this, we start to trust in our ability to right a wrong rather than in God's ability. When we attack others we are out of the will of God and open to yet a greater attack of the enemy. If with each ensuing attack we continue to blame people, we soon stop asking God what we should say or do. We can even come to the place where we blame God for our situation. This interferes with our relationship to God. If we aren't in communion through prayer with God, we will lose that trusting relationship needed to keep our faith active and expanding.

What is the solution to this third temptation designed to dismantle our faith? The first thing we must do is to acknowledge our need to repent of our own ways and acknowledge God's control over us. Our second step is to ask the Holy Spirit to give us God's view of the situation and then ask Him to bring His solution to pass. In other words, lay aside your ideas and solutions. Thirdly, you must recognize that you are not your own defender. God is your Defender, your Shield and your Vindicator! You are not called to respond to people, but to God. When you do so, He is able to use you to reach others. In Isaiah 59:19 we are promised that:

> "When the enemy shall come, like a flood the Spirit of the Lord will lift up a standard against him

and put him to flight — for He will come like a
rushing stream which the breath of the Lord drives.
He shall come as a Redeemer to Zion and to those in
Jacob (Israel) who turn from transgression, says the
Lord. (AMP)

If we have indeed repented of our own ways the
following scripture encompasses, in a large part, all that
we need in order to maintain a proper attitude:

If then you have been raised up with Christ, keep
seeking the things above, where Christ is, seated at
the right hand of God.

Set your mind on the things above, not on the
things that are on earth.

For you have died and your life is hidden with
Christ in God.

When Christ, who is our life, is revealed, then you
also will be revealed with Him in glory.

Therefore consider the members of your earthly
body as dead to immorality, impurity, passion, evil
desire, and greed, which amounts to idolatry.

For it is on account of these things that the wrath of
God will come, and in them you also once walked,
when you were living in them.

But now you also, put them all aside: anger, wrath,
malice, slander, and abusive speech from your mouth.

Do not lie to one another, since you laid aside the
old self with its evil practices, and have put on the new
self who is being renewed to a true knowledge

according to the image of the One who created him...
(Colossians 3:1-10, NAS)

This scripture is one of our best counterattacks, for through its truths we see who we are, who God is, and what He is doing on our behalf. Notice verses two and three: "Set your mind on the things above, not on the things that are on earth. For you have died and your life is hidden with Christ in God." These verses tell us where we should be looking and to Whom. By reminding ourselves that we are dead to ourselves and alive in Christ Jesus, we will not be moved from our trust in God by situations, people, hurts, persecutions or our emotions. Our decision to set our minds on the spiritual realm (the realm where God's perspective has preeminence) and its truth will keep the gift of faith activated.

It's really quite simple: if we set our minds on the things above, we know that God is trustworthy, but if we set our minds on the things below, we begin to question God's ability and willingness to act. In other words, we see all the wrongs that do indeed exist, but by never looking to the things above, we will never find the solutions.

I am reminded of the old song, "What A Friend".[3] One line that is quickened to me talks about the pain we often suffer, of the needless burden we bear, all because we do not carry everything to God in prayer. This will happen if we do not put on our new nature.

As you read the account of David's life in the Old Testament, you will notice that one characteristic stands out about his attitudes. He was a man who honored God by honoring God's anointed (Saul) even though Saul was continually trying to kill him. He continually forgave King Saul for these acts of terror.[4] This constant assault would prove the fiber of David's character and heart.[5] This would be crucial, for God selected David's lineage to be that of Jesus.[6] In the same way, our fiber, character and attitudes are strengthened and re-aligned properly in our struggles and trials. We grow, like David, to quickly implement the principles of obedience, repentance, forgiveness, or worship in order to stay in close fellowship with God. This in turn activates our gift of faith.

OUR SELF-WILL

The fourth thing that keeps our faith from remaining active is the lack of its use. As with any gift from God, faith can become dormant from lack of use. There is a difference between dormant and dead. To be dormant is to be alive but not actively producing anything. We've talked of this same effect with regard to meditation.

When we as Christians activate our *self-will* we cause our gift of faith to become dormant. Allowing our self-will to rule over God's will always produces sorrow in our lives and leaves us feeling hopeless. If we know that submitting to God's will produces peace, joy, and hope, it makes sense to go with His will. Jesus always allowed the will of His Father to have preeminence in Him. As a result, Jesus demonstrated what actively producing faith was. The manifestation of His faith caused the world to resound with news of the miraculous! This pleased the Father, and I know that it is our desire to please Him, too. Let's not grieve the Father by diminishing or ignoring this marvelous gift of faith He's given us.

By allowing God to operate and activate this gift of faith in and through us, we not only please Him, but we also allow the other gifts He has placed within us to become active.

For example, in my own life, I have chosen to allow God to use me as His vessel or servant. As a result, I'm not the same Bible teacher that I was ten years ago. God has expanded this gift because I have continued to choose to let Him. At the same time, God has been expanding the gift of teaching, the gift of faith placed within me has been expanded through more and more opportunities to trust Him. I perceive more of Him; I know Him better than I knew Him ten years ago. I trust Him more, because I have seen Him active in my life. I have a greater understanding of the long-range vision God has given me than I have ever had before, and this is simply because I have chosen to continue to flow with Him and with His will.

LOCK INTO HIS WAY

So what is the solution to keeping your God-given faith active and to put situations, circumstances, emotions, hurts and persecution in their place? Take the position ordained for you by God. Your position is to be hidden in Christ. Speak to everything that would threaten your confidence in God and His provision by speaking the name of Jesus over them. The scripture says the name of Jesus is above everything that is named, and so you have the authority to use His name. Make a decision to stay in a position of victory instead of being defeated by your own failures (eg. Peter's denying Jesus three times) or circumstances. Make this decision based on what Jesus said in Matthew 28:18 — "All authority has been given to Me in heaven and on earth..." — and be controlled by His power.

PART II

The Enemies of Our Faith

DEMONS OF DESTRUCTION

In John 10:10 Jesus states that Satan comes to kill, to rob and to destroy. In other words, he wants us to be put in a position of despair. Satan uses his evil forces to come against us to work this destruction. He uses fear, failure to forgive and anger towards God and its devastating effects. All these weapons are found in his arsenal.

How does Satan bring about his destruction, since he is not omnipresent like God? Satan takes his fallen angels and assigns them over us to do his dirty work. Our abundance in God's promise and our trust in Him can be rendered inactive if we aren't aware of how to stop the fallen angels' activities in our lives. They are assigned to rob us of our peace, our joy and our sense of righteousness. If Satan can steal those things, it is very hard to trust, rely, depend and lean upon God. If we don't have a sense of righteousness, we won't feel worthy to come into the presence of God; then we do not sense His peace and the joy of the Lord. And this in turn saps our strength, because the Word says that the joy of the Lord is our strength! Without a sense of righteousness and peace our joy is nonexistent.

This knowledge could be very distressing if our God had not provided an arsenal of His own for our defense. In Hebrews 1:14 we are told that God has provided us with ministering spirits (angels) to render service for the sake of those who will inherit salvation. In other words, God brings part of His abundance through the spiritual forces loyal to Him.

In addition to God's ministering angels, we have the name of Jesus. We've already discussed our authority in the name of Jesus, so we simply use that authority and command every demon assigned over us to stop its activity — we order them in the name of Jesus to shut up and we speak confusion into every plan or strategy they want to use against us. We ask God to send His ministering spirits to care for us and to help us in our resistance of the enemy. We ask the Holy Spirit to release His power for our defense.

BONDAGE OF FEAR

If we have used our authority to bind the evil forces assigned over us and we are still experiencing a lack of righteousness, peace, and joy, then we need to check three areas that would produce the same result.

We must ask ourselves if we have fear of any kind. Fear is the opposite of peace, so it can be used as a powerful weapon against us. Fear of man, fear of rejection, fear of the unknown, and fear of failure can all shut down our active faith.

How do we deal with these fears? If we continue to

replay these fears in our minds, we become bound by them. Our solution to rid ourselves of fear is to speak to our Father God in prayer about these fears. We can say, "Father, I have a fear of rejection and I know that You did not give me a spirit of fear (I Timothy 2:7), so I'm giving this fear to You. Now Father, replace it with your peace, in Jesus' name. Amen."

II Corinthians 10:3-6 declares that these fears are lofty things and speculations which are against the knowledge of God and His power. The fears we experience have their origin in our enemy and his forces. Fears become strong-holds and can be removed only by an act of obedience to God, rather than by continuing to embrace them. What is this act of obedience He seeks from us? God desires that we take Him at His word. Is not the God of the Universe greater than any fear? Isn't He able to take that fear from us and give us great confidence and peace in Himself? The Father is not only able, but willing to help when we call upon Him (Psalms 107). God has given us mighty weapons for use against the enemy. Paul says these weapons are divinely powerful (Ephesians 6). God has promised that His power will be displayed in our midst through these weapons. The most powerful weapon we have is the name of Jesus! After we've prayed to our Father, then we can speak the name of Jesus over any fear and it has to go! If it tries to come back, don't let it have a foothold. Speak to that fear and remind it that it's been put under the name of Jesus and that the Father has already taken it from us.

IMPRISONED BY OUR OWN EXPECTATIONS

Satan also comes against us through anger and frustration. Anger and frustration deactivate our faith. Sometimes we get angry when the timing of the Lord is not understood, or because our scope of the situation is narrow and we haven't consulted God for His revelation and solution. We need to ask God to widen our vision of the situation to His view instead of ours.

I recall a time in my life when I was greatly frustrated by the fact that I felt very distant from God. Shortly after this, our family went to a Thursday night service. When the service started I entered into the worship and praise out of obedience, not out of a great sense of God's presence. Finally I said, "God! I can't sense your presence, I feel my prayers are empty, what's going on?" What happened next I can only describe as a spiritual vision. I didn't see this vision with my natural eyes, I saw it with my spiritual eyes. Jesus was holding a small child in His arms. Suddenly, I realized that the little child was me. Then He spoke. "Jackie, what do you see?" I was looking over Jesus' shoulder and I said, "I see a beautiful sphere of blue and white with patches of green. Lord, what is it?" Jesus replied, "It's the world as I see it. Jackie, you've let all the things around you govern you. Stay in my arms and you will always see things as I do and you will always sense My presence and love." I can truthfully say that when I've done as Jesus instructed me, I've not only seen His solutions, but I've been completely confident in His timing!

Another way frustration and anger take hold of us is through our expectations. We expect others to act in a Godly manner. When they don't or when we see the imperfection of our world around us, we become frustrated and angry. What we are really saying is, "God, why don't You do something?" The imperfection and the destruction we see around us is not a product of God, but of Satan. Don't let Satan dismantle the gift of faith because of your disappointment in this world. We need to focus on the way God is showing us to walk and walk in that way. If God has control over us, we'll not be controlled by the world and its imperfections. Start walking under His control by choosing to relinquish this anger toward God, others, or circumstances and ask the Holy Spirit to work His forgiveness in you. Don't place any expectations on people or things, but rely on God and His promises.

Look at David's life as portrayed in the Old Testament; he was anointed as king of Israel while Saul was still officially king. David relied upon God to manifest in the natural what He had declared in the supernatural. David had wisdom to know that to place a time limit on God would produce expectations and expectations would cause him to sin against God.

David's wisdom came from above and we have the same wisdom through the power of the Holy Spirit who dwells within us. We can't let ourselves be imprisoned by expectations which cause us to sin. Like David, we must *not* allow the enemy of our souls to keep our faith inactive through false expectations. We must be quick to repent and be pure in heart before our Father God. In this way, our communion with God is uninterrupted and the Holy Spirit is able to nurture us. He is able to keep our trust and reliance on God constant.

ROOTS OF UNFORGIVENESS

Jesus speaks to us about another area that affects our sense of righteousness, peace, joy and faith. I know that I have spoken about this matter before, but it bears repeating. In Matthew 6:14-15, Jesus says that to fail to forgive is sin and that if we don't forgive others, God cannot forgive us... In other words, failure to forgive others will hurt us, not others. We hurt our relationship with our heavenly Father because we're in a state of sin, and that separates us from God. Failure to forgive produces within us some very nasty roots. The longer we stay in unforgiveness, the longer bitterness and resentment continue to live with us and grow in strength. It becomes harder and harder to truly forgive others. Since we have separated ourselves from God and others by unforgiveness, we have also shut our gift of faith down.

What is the solution? Do what Jesus says: forgive others so that God can forgive you. Re-order your thinking. Recognize unforgiveness as sin and look upon it as deadly. If someone put a loaded gun to your head would *you* pull the trigger? Of course not! When someone hurts you, that's the loaded gun placed against your head. If your enemy can convince you that you're justified in not forgiving someone, you have just pulled the trigger! This illustration may seem drastic, but my desire is that you see graphically the power of sin in any form and flee from it! (II Tim. 2:22)

CHAPTER IV

Reactivating Our Faith

Many times we as Christians experience a high-water mark in the activation of our faith. We sense we're moving along in a smooth fashion with the things of God and our trust in Him seems impenetrable. We rejoice that we are so blessed. Then suddenly something happens and we're not sure we want to even try to move on with God. The following illustration may be helpful for you to understand what I'm saying:

Let's say a child is riding his bicycle, and another child decides to play a mean trick by putting a stick through the spokes of the moving wheel. The child on the bicycle is thrown off and suffers skinned elbows, knees and several nasty bruises. This would be a very unpleasant experience for him, and he would very likely be hesitant to get back on his bicycle. He would remember what happened before. He'd reason that if it happened once, it could happen again. Even though he had loved riding the bicycle before, he'd give up riding and retreat to his room. What the child would fail to realize is that the bicycle was not to blame for his injuries. He was injured because another child submitted to an evil thought.

In the same way, we as Christians can decide our "bicycle" walk with God is too much to bear because we've experienced harm done when an evil action was committed by others or by us.

Many times we as Christians suffer greatly after we have made a decision to follow Jesus and do all that He has commanded us. We come away from an encounter with our old nature or Satan and are so discouraged and so battle-scarred we just can't pick up the call to *trust and obey*. We feel totally beaten and are not sure we can endure another attack or defeat.

This is a normal response to our experience, but we need not stay bound by this experience. This aspect of our walk of faith is not something we relish because, by nature, we like to have everything laid out in a neat package. When we are suffering, disappointed, or fail, we want to say, "No, God, no more!" We want to say, "God, I tried and look what happened!" We sometimes feel that we're the only ones who've ever experienced something so devastating.

Alfred Ebersheim in his book, *OLD TESTAMENT BIBLE HISTORY*, made this statement on faith well over 100 years ago: "But this is the very test of faith — that the past never seems to afford a quite sufficient basis for it, but that it must always stretch beyond our former experience, just because it is always a *present act*, the outcome of a *present life*."

I feel Ebersheim has hit upon two keys to moving on

with God in this statement. He states that faith is a *present act* which results from a *present life*.

When our family first came to know the Lord personally, we moved in the things of God with great enthusiasm! We had experienced the release of the Holy Spirit and were blessed with many brothers and sisters in Christ. Though we all had a great zeal for God and a longing to serve Him, we knew very little about our enemy. We had little idea of his strategies and how subtle he could be in his work of destruction. We knew nothing of what would happen if we tried to live our lives as we had before our rebirth. Unknown to most of us, some in our community were deliberately walking outside of God's will as expressed in the Bible. Many of us were simply not prepared for the attacks that came as a result.

Because we were in a state of ignorance, we became easy prey. When the assault was successful in bringing destruction into several lives within our community of believers, we were so devastated that we *felt* too paralyzed to counterattack. Some of our precious brothers and sisters had been seduced into returning to the world's ways. Everything in our lives seemed to become a maze. Nothing was crystal clear anymore. We had grown to love these people and our hearts ached to see them return to God and His mercy. His mercy had an immediate effect, but none of our prayers had a visible effect. We felt disillusioned, crushed and betrayed both by our wayward brothers and sisters and by God Himself.

Somehow each of us would have to come to terms with the loss of this battle to Satan. The determining factor for each of us would be our faith. This determining factor would outweigh the defeat of each believer according to how each reacted or responded to the situation and to God.

We found ourselves having to deal with anger toward our fellow believers for being "duped" by Satan. Anger towards God also set in for "letting" it happen. (Am I hitting some common chords with some of you who are reading this?) Like it or not, it was decision time for us all! The very core of our faith was shaken as we struggled to place our trust in God in spite of the circumstances. Our faith (trust, reliance upon) in God would be our only avenue out.

Since we were in the middle of this situation, we could observe and monitor the effects of the various responses of the community of believers. Some saints never ventured out again, returning to the Christian life as they knew it before they were empowered by the Holy Spirit. Some held fast to their state of growth before the enemy's attack while others forged ahead, not willing to let one battle lost *deprive* them of the overall victory God has promised. The latter group has *applied* the two keys that Ebersheim spoke of long ago. 1) They live in the *present*, still saying "yes" to God, and 2) They continue to forget those things that lie behind (the experience of pain), pressing on and drawing from the past only that which will cause them to stay in the *present* (Philippians 3:13-14).

Expecting God to act in the *present* is the key to trusting and obeying Him. Dealing with anger and hurts from the past is necessary if we are to put those things behind us and advance to the present.

It is the tactic of the enemy to attack all Christian endeavors, but he keeps us in defeat only if we remain in a state of anger, resentment, or bitterness toward others or God. I don't know exactly what the other saints did in their situation, but our family made a decision to forgive, to love, and to continue our prayers for those ensnared by the enemy. This freed us to move on with God. Forgiveness has freed us to live in the *present* so we can continue to see His *present* acts in our lives and the lives of others.

Do you remember I said that we felt crushed because our prayers for these people seemed to have no effect? Well, some of those people have returned to God. God has heard our prayers, but God knew what had to transpire in their lives before the answer could be made manifest.

If you *walk* with God for any length of time, you will experience the attacks of the enemy. With each attack you will have a decision to make. If you choose to return to where you were before your relationship with God began, or to "tread water" where you are in your Christian walk, this will not produce the full and abundant life promised by Jesus (John 10:10). Our family has observed the consequences of these decisions in the lives of several brothers and sisters. It is very sad to see that the present life they lead is underdeveloped spiritually or that their faith has become dormant with neglect.

Now, here's the good news! If you find yourself in a place where the enemy has shut down your active faith in

God, the Father has a way to overcome. God wants to bring you to your feet, to stand tall, and be full of strength (His strength). The Holy Spirit wants to build up what has been torn down, so you can once again rely, depend, trust, adhere to and be confident in Him. The Father wants you once again to experience the freedom of soaring with Him in His dimension.

Look to His Word and you will see that He is aware of your circumstances and that He has already made provision for you:

Be of sober spirit, be on the alert. Your adversary, the devil, prowls about like a roaring lion, seeking someone to devour. But resist him, firm in your faith, knowing that the same experiences of suffering are being accomplished by your brethren who are in the world. And after you have suffered for a little, the God of all grace, who called you to His eternal glory in Christ, will Himself perfect, confirm, strengthen, and establish you. (I Peter 5:8-10, NAS).

He has the following promises for those of us who, as His disciples, need to be lifted up in order to move again:

For the Lord God helps Me, therefore I am not disgraced; therefore, I have set My face like flint, and I know that I shall not be ashamed. He who vindicates Me is near; who will contend with Me? Let us stand up to each other; Who has a case against Me? Let him draw near to Me. Behold, the Lord helps Me; Behold, they will all wear out like a garment; the moth will eat them. Who is among you that fears the Lord, That obeys the voice of His servant, that walks in darkness and has no light? Let him trust in the name of the Lord and rely on his God. (Isaiah 50:4-10, NAS)

Surely, thus says the Lord, 'Even the captives of the mighty man will be taken away, and the prey of the tyrant will be rescued; for I will contend with the one who contends with you, and I will save your sons.' (Isaiah 49:25 NAS)

We also have the fabulous circle of God's fire surrounding us, and He says His glory dwells in our midst (Zechariah 2:5).

Realize what the circle or wall of fire is doing for us. It is protecting us from without. It is keeping the darts of the enemy from overtaking us. God is so multi-faceted in His power that He is purifying us within also. By so doing, He is able to come in all His glory and dwell in our midst.

Do you know what the glory of God is? It is the manifested presence of the *very person* of God Himself! Now that's something to shout about! Just think, Emmanuel is *literally* God with us. If God is with us, then He is more than able to strengthen us and establish us.

If we experience God strengthening us, our trust and reliance upon Him becomes established in us and we will not retreat, but advance! Our God, who gives us our strength and our power will always keep us!

Now if we know that God's full intent is to keep us

strong in our faith, He is able to give us the wisdom to remove anything that is hindering our gift of faith from being active. This wisdom will come as we pray and ask the Holy Spirit to reveal any blocks that are interrupting our trust in God.

He will also let us know where we're living in past failures, fears or hurts that block our lives in the present. The Holy Spirit is willing and waiting to bring us into the *present*, for it is only in the present that we can see our faith in God expanding. This expansion is made possible by using experiences of our past as positive stepping stones to the *present*.

Just as Ebersheim stated, that past never quite prepares us for the next step of faith, but it can cause us to trust that the unknown is known by God and that God will do what He's promised.

If you sense that you're not living in the present, expecting God's *present* acts, you'll need to apply the principles outlined in Chapter II, "Activating Your Faith." Let's briefly review these principles.

COMMUNING WITH GOD IS A MUST!

The definition of communion is to have communication, intercourse or an exchange of ideas or thoughts. What ideas or thoughts is God desirous of communicating to us? The Father desires that we keep our faith in Him active. How do we know this? Notice that all of the scripture referred to in this chapter relates to what God will do for us to ensure that His gift of faith remains active in us. How will this be accomplished? We will start our life in the present, using present faith, by being in constant communication with God. The communication between God and us will come through the power of the Holy Spirit speaking to our hearts, which makes God's promises real to us. By the Holy Spirit quickening the Word of God to our understanding, we see His promises come alive in us.

READ AND MEDITATE UPON THE WORD OF GOD

The Bible says the Word was in the beginning and the Word was God. It is just as important for us to read and mediate upon the Word of God as to commune with Him personally. The Word of God reveals more of Him to us. When we've been devastated by an attack of Satan, it's easy to lay aside our Bibles. Saints, that's just what our enemy wants. If we do not have input from God through prayer and His Word, Satan can have our minds to himself. He can feed us his lies and we might buy them, since nothing else has been put in to counter his thoughts. This is a very dangerous place to be found.

Keep the Word of God ever before your eyes that you may gain wisdom, for in wisdom you gain His strength.

PLEASE DON'T SOLO

Would you consider getting into a small plane and taking off without an instructor or training? Heavens, no! In the same way, we are never expected to solo in our walk with God. We are never expected to activate our gift of faith solo. As Christians, we are inseparable from God.

Jesus said to invite Him into our hearts and He would come abide (live) in us and we in Him forever. If He (Jesus) is living in us, then we are never alone. In Jesus is the fulness of the Deity, so we will never lack for the power that works within us to see God's *present acts* (active faith) in our *present* lives. "For I am confident of this very thing, that He who began a good work in you will perfect it until the day of Christ" (Philippians 1:6, NAS). We are assured that to be hidden in Christ is to have your Defender, your Vindicator, and your Deliverer bonded to you no matter what!

FREELY LOVE AND FREELY FORGIVE OTHERS

Since it is God who is going to shape us, form us, and defend us from within, Jesus being in us, we are free to love with the Godly love through Christ. In the same way, we are free to forgive with Godly forgiveness.

You may be thinking this sounds like a nice thing to do, but how do you love and forgive with God's kind of love and forgiveness? As an act of our will we give God permission to let His love and forgiveness flow through us. When we acknowledge we are unable to love or forgive with our own power and we ask the Holy Spirit to come and work love and forgiveness in us, then we succeed. This success causes our faith to be reactivated because we see the hand of the Lord move in us, transforming our thoughts, emotions, and attitudes to agree with His.

The knowledge of this came to me through a personal experience a few months ago. Suddenly I realized that as I would go to teach a Bible study, I would feel uneasy, as if I wasn't honestly living what I was teaching. The enemy does bring condemnation, but I sensed that was not the case in this incident.

After seeking the Lord about this I was still at a loss until I finally said, "Lord, I can't go on, please help me!" Within the next two days, I was put into contact with a lady who helped me to see what was going on. None of us would like to hear what she said, for she was very candid. She said, "Jackie, you are in unforgiveness; you are in sin." I quickly reviewed my attitudes and just as quickly the Holy Spirit showed me she was right on the money. I had made a mental decision to forgive and I felt I'd even chosen to forgive as an act of my will, but these alone won't cut it! I quickly repented of this sin, but still felt heavy laden. Then she explained the key that I'd missed: letting God work His forgiveness in me toward others.

I felt like the Galatians that Paul admonished (Galatians 3) when he called them foolish because they had started in the works of the Spirit and had returned to the works of flesh. That's exactly what I had done. Having so much knowledge of what I was to do, I had forgotten that nothing works without the Holy Spirit's power. No will-power or mind-power can truly forgive.

Any time sin has a foothold, our perspective becomes warped. Because of this sin, I was in judgment of others. I had not knowingly stayed in sin, but once it was pointed out to me, I asked God to remove it from me quickly. As I prayed a prayer to allow the true forgiveness of God to flow, I sensed the weight lift and the peace of God return. When I returned to teaching the next time, all vestiges of this sin and its burdens were gone!

Through this experience, I learned how easily I could become corrupted by sin as well as the value of forbearance of others. Understanding Godly forgiveness has helped me to continue in my walk with God.

FORBEARING ONE ANOTHER IN LOVE

All of us as Christians have seen members of the body of Christ discredit Him, or we have had personal differences with other Christians. If we are to avoid corruption by judgment or conflicts which affect our walk of faith, we'll need to learn forbearance with love:

> ... and have put on the new self who is being renewed to a true knowledge according to the image of the One who created him.
>
> — a renewal in which there is no distinction between Greek and Jew, circumcised and uncircumcised, barbarian, Scythian, slave and freeman, but Christ is all, and in all.
>
> And so, as those who have been chosen of God, holy and beloved, put on a heart of compassion, kindness, humility, gentleness, and patience;
>
> bearing [forbearing] with one another, and forgiving each other, whoever has a complaint against anyone; just as the Lord forgave you, so also should you.
>
> And beyond all these things put on love, which is the perfect bond of unity. (Colossians 3:10-14, NAS)

In Vine's *Expository Dictionary of New Testament Words* we find this definition of forbearance: "Long-suffering is that quality of self-restraint in the face of provocation which does not hastily retaliate or promptly punish; it is the opposite of anger and is associated with mercy, and is used of God, Ex. 34:6, Rom. 2:4; I Pet. 3:20. Patience is the quality that does not surrender to circumstances or succumb under trial; it is the opposite of despondency and is associated with hope...." Vine's also describes it as *enduring* or *to bear* with *gentleness* or *clemency*. Paul prefaces his comments on forbearance with the instructions to put on, as the elect of God, hearts of mercies, kindness, humbleness of mind, meekness, and longsuffering.

God knew we would experience difficulty in both the areas of disappointment in our fellow Christians' conduct and personality conflicts. This is why Paul was inspired to prepare us before the need arose for forbearance so we would be able to maintain the unity God desires. Godly unity will be realized as we put on the bond of love.

Throughout this scripture (Col. 3:10-14), Paul stresses that we should put on the new self, put on a heart of compassion, kindness, humility, gentleness, and patience, put on love. Read on in verse 16 where Paul admonishes us not to forsake the gathering together of the body of Christ. We need to follow through with the putting on of all Paul said first. By putting on all of these, we will walk in forbearance and forgiveness. Only in this way will we be able to come together in the spirit that God intended.

Forbearing one another is not always easy, but it is required! I once heard a minister tell about his travels to many countries. Each time he would come to a new church with their own doctrines, they would try to get him baptized their way. He found a very gentle way to decline at each church without bringing offense to his brethren.

This is what God wants of us. If we won't forbear one another in love our revelation of God and of the body of Christ will be seriously hampered. Our faith will not operate because our focus will be on the imperfections or inaccuracy of our fellow Christians. This is judgment, and judgment for us is sin. Oh, we want to avoid this pit! The Holy Spirit will always give us the way to forbear or forgive in love if we allow Him to work His transformation in us.

TARES AMONG THE WHEAT

He presented another parable to them saying, "The kingdom of heaven may be compared to a man who sowed good seed in his field.

"But while men were sleeping, his enemy came and sowed tares also among the wheat, and went away.

"But when the wheat sprang up and bore grain, then the tares became evident also.

"And the slaves of the landowner came and said to him, 'Sir, did you not sow good seed in your field? How then does it have tares?'

"And he said to them, 'An enemy has done this!'

"And the slaves said to him, 'Do you want us, then, to go and gather them up?'

"But he said, 'No, lest while you are gathering up the tares, you may root up the wheat with them.

" 'Allow both to grow together until the harvest; and in the time of harvest I will say to the reapers, "First gather up the tares and bind them in bundles to burn them up; but gather the wheat into my barn." ' "

... Then He left the multitudes, and went into the house. And His disciples came to Him, saying, "Explain to us the parable of the tares of the field."

And He answered and said, "The one who sows the good seed is the Son of Man,

"and the field is the world; and as for the good seed, these are the sons of the kingdom; and the tares are the sons of the evil one;

"and the enemy who sowed them is the devil, and the harvest is the end of the age; and the reapers are angels.

"Therefore just as the tares are gathered up and burned with fire, so shall it be at the end of the age.

"The Son of Man will send forth His angels, and they will gather out of His kingdom all stumbling blocks, and those who commit lawlessness,

"and will cast them into the furnace of fire; in that place there shall be weeping and gnashing of teeth.

"Then the righteous will shine forth as the sun in

the kingdom of their Father. He who has ears, let him hear." (Matthew 13:24,30, 36-43 NAS)

Why did the sower of the good seed say an enemy had planted the tares? This parable had great spiritual overtones as we shall see as we discover the answer.

First, let's find out what tares are as defined by *Dicken's New Analytical Bible and Dictionary of the Bible*: "A weed, or bearded darnel, that in the blade state could not be distinguished from wheat but in the ear state was quite dissimilar and could then be easily separated."

Vine's Expository Dictionary says, "Tares:.....as tall as wheat and resembling wheat in appearance. The seeds are poisonous to man and herbivorous animals, producing sleepiness, nausea, convulsions and even death."

The Lord describes the tares as "the sons of the evil one."

Earlier, I said we are to forbear one another in love. Paul was talking about our conduct toward true brothers and sisters in Christ, but what do we do with those who come as tares? In Jesus' parable He is the man who sowed the wheat, so He is the one who decides what to do with the tares. He says to wait until harvest time and they'll be clearly revealed as tares. The workers are the body of Christ who follow His orders. The tares are all who belong to the evil one inside and outside the church. He further stated that it will be His angels who do the separating, not us. However, He does have something He wants us to do while we wait for the harvest.

A study of wheat and tares in the natural growth to maturity will reveal why Jesus used this illustration to help explain our place in the present world. As one definition stated, at first the blades of wheat and tares look exactly alike. But as they mature the difference becomes quite obvious: wheat remains golden in color and full of a white heart, while tares turn black and are hollow inside. In the same fashion, Jesus says the angels assigned to the harvest will clearly know who's who.

Spiritually speaking, Jesus is saying He'll come back and direct the separation process. In the meantime, we are to protect ourselves with the wisdom given us through the Word and the Spirit.

Jesus tells us how to operate in this wisdom through the means of two more parables which follow the parable of the tares and wheat. In them He reveals the ways to avoid corruption.

In the parable of the leavened bread, He says to watch for the leaven (leaven stood for evil). Jesus is telling us we'll not be free of false teachings, but we do not have to let them infiltrate us (Matthew 16:6-12).

In His parable of the mustard seed He's saying the church will start out very small, but grow to great proportions. Because of this great growth, birds will come and nest in the church. Birds were also a symbol for evil.[7] We will not be free of evil forces moving in our midst any more than wheat can be free of tares, but this does not have to discourage or corrupt us. We are seeds of wheat, and wheat we will remain. Just as natural wheat mixed with tares continues to grow, we will continue to grow because our eyes are on the Sower and the Harvester of our spirits, the sower and harvester who is also the Author and Finisher of our faith (Matthew 13:31-32).

CHAPTER V

The Operation of Our Faith

PART I

Intrepreting the Voice of the Holy Spirit

Our faith operates through a series of stages:

1. Receiving a personal word from God
2. Trusting what we've heard to be from God
3. Resting in the knowledge that we can lean upon the Father
4. Yielding all to God so that He will be free to move on our behalf.

This chapter will address these various stages and help you to identify them. The checklist above will be found throughout this chapter in order to help you note the progress. With this checklist of progression, you'll be able to see how the Holy Spirit is moving and how the principles of faith's activation are operative in your life.

First, we need to know how to hear the voice of the Holy Spirit in order to move into Stage I of the operation of our faith.

INTERPRETING THE VOICE OF THE HOLY SPIRIT

When you watch television, you are incorporating two of your five senses. Your eyes view the image on the screen and your ears listen to what is being spoken. Next, your mind quickly sorts the images received with your eyes and the sounds heard with your ears. As your mind combines the two, you are then able to understand what you are seeing and hearing.

In the same way, we can understand what the Holy Spirit is speaking only if we use the faculties which God has given us. In our case, however, we combine our natural faculties with the supernatural.

Let's first read Acts 2:4: "And they were all filled with the Holy Spirit and began to speak with other tongues, as the Spirit was giving them utterance" (NAS).

Notice that Paul says, "*they spoke,*" so the first natural faculties they used were their voices, which were able to be heard by others, as well as by themselves. The next thing Paul says in this portion of scripture is "*as the Holy Spirit gave utterance.*" In other words, the Holy Spirit created the sounds which produced the words they spoke. The words were supernatural. As they spoke the supernatural words the Holy Spirit had ordained, their ears could hear these supernatural words also.

The disciples had two inputs: the speaking of the Holy Spirit's words and the hearing of the Holy Spirit's words. But how did they get these supernatural words interpreted into their natural words which brought understanding?

As I was praying one day, the voice of the Father began to speak to my spirit. Our communion time started with the Father's asking me a question. "Jackie, tell Me, when you come into My throne room what do you do?" I said, "Oh Father, I bow before You, I worship You, and I listen to everything You say." The Father said, "That's right! Now what do you do when My Son speaks to you?" I said, "Father, I bow my knee to My Lord, I worship Him, and I listen to everything He says." Then the Father said, "That's right. Now, tell Me, Jackie, what do you do when the Holy Spirit speaks?" A sudden, sweeping realization came over me that I had not reverenced the Holy Spirit in the same manner. I began to weep as I realized I'd grieved the third person of the Godhead. I knew instantly why I'd grieved Him. I, like many others, had experienced the release of the Holy Spirit in my life and I had submitted my faculties to Him so that He could speak His heavenly language through my voice that I might hear His spoken words.[8] Like many, I had experienced what I thought was a wonderful phenomenon. At the same time the Holy Spirit was speaking, I could be thinking about something else with my mind. In other words, my mind was doing its own thing. I would never have come into the throne room of God and thought of not listening to Him, but that's exactly what I was doing to the precious Holy Spirit. What irreverence!

I said, "Oh! Father, forgive me, I have sinned. Teach me

to listen and reverence the Holy Spirit in the same way I reverence and listen to Your voice and the voice of My Lord."

Out of my own need the Father graciously instructed me and gave me the keys I needed in order to reverence and listen to the voice of the Holy Spirit.

The following instructions were given to me by the Father: "Require your mind and ears to listen to what is being spoken by My Holy Spirit." "Oh," I thought, "that's easy!" As the Holy Spirit's utterances came forth from my mouth, I started to listen with my ears and mind. I was so disappointed when it didn't work! What was wrong? The Father is so loving and patient. He said, "Jackie, once you've submitted your will to listen, you'll need to use the authority of My Son's name to bring your mind and ears into submission.

I spoke to my mind and ears and said, "Mind and ears, in the name of Jesus, I require you to listen to everything the Holy Spirit is speaking."

As I've continued to submit my will and speak the authoritative name of Jesus over my mind and ears I've seen results! The results did not come overnight, however; they were realized over a period of time. The revering and adhering to the voice of the Holy Spirit has also required a continuous vigil in order to honor God, to be built up in faith and to do His will. If this sounds like work, it is, but the benefits are tremendous!

When we follow the Father's instructions, He is able to take our natural faculties (our ears and minds) and His supernatural faculties (the words of the Holy Spirit) to bring to our understanding His will and way for us. Let me explain: As the Holy Spirit speaks His heavenly language through us, and we listen with our natural ears and minds, God is able to transfer through our submitted wills an interpretation of what the Holy Spirit is praying or saying. This mechanism is of God's own supernatural design for us.

This is one of the ways God demonstrates what Paul writes of in Romans 8:14 and 16.

> For all who are being led by the Spirit of God, these are sons of God. (Romans 8:14, NAS)
> The Spirit Himself bears witness with our spirit that we are children of God, ... (Romans 8:16, NAS)

All of us, as Christians, long to know the voice of God, to understand His ways, to become intimately acquainted with Him. All of us long to honor our God. All these desires can be fulfilled as we come before Him with reverential awe of the Holy Spirit. When we bow our knee to Him and listen to everything that He speaks, be it through His heavenly language or through an inward witness, we will know His voice.

PART II

The Operation of Faith

STAGE I

A Specific Word from God

Keep in mind as you read the rest of this chapter that this is not a formula to follow to make your faith operate, but a description of how to observe it in operation. It's somewhat like getting a package of flower seeds. On the back of the package you read how to plant and water the seeds. Then the information continues to tell you what to expect. It tells you what the first blade will look like, how tall it will grow, how long before it should blossom, what color, etc. Once you've planted the seeds, you'll be an observer of God's creative power in operation.

In the same way, once you've said "yes" to a word the Father has spoken to you, He will direct the entire operation of your faith. This chapter is just a description of what you'll be observing in God's creative operation of the gift of faith within you. Please do not take these stages and try to use them as steps of instruction. These stages are brought to fullness by the Holy Spirit. Just as a seed cannot cause itself to grow, we cannot cause faith's operation to occur. Our role is to avoid uprooting the "yes" seed planted in us. The previous chapter was devoted to the ways in which we cause the seed to stay planted.

In the third chapter of Galatians, we see how the operation of faith is facilitated and by Whom.

Galatians 3:5-6:

> Does He then, who provides you with the Spirit and works miracles among you do it by the works of the Law, or by hearing with faith? Even so Abraham believed God, and it was reckoned to him as righteousness. (NAS)

In Galatians 3:5-7, we are told that because we trust, adhere, rely, depend and cleave to what the Father has spoken to us through the gift of the marvelous Holy Spirit, we will be called the sons of righteousness, the true sons of Abraham. We are also told that it is only by faith that this is accomplished. We've already established the fact that all people are given that gift of faith, so what we need now is to understand its actual operation, so that we may cooperate with the Holy Spirit in bringing our faith to maturity. Hearing a word from God alone will not bring this maturity, but acting upon what you hear will. Acting is planting your "Yes, Lord" seed.

As stated earlier in Part I of this chapter, the first thing that must happen if we are to see the operation of faith occur in our lives is to hear a word from God specifically for us as individuals. This is why Part I is so important. This is a prerequisite to the operation of faith. Abraham heard a very specific word from God, and this was the beginning of the operation of faith in his life (Genesis 12:1-4).

STAGE II

Trusting the Word You've Heard

Let's study the definitions of each of the words describing faith. In this way, we will gain a clear understanding of how we should react to the spoken words of God which are meant for us.

TRUST — 1. Assured reliance on some person or thing; a confident dependence on the character, ability, strength, or truth of someone or something: Belief

2. A person or thing in which confidence is placed: a basis of reliance, faith or hope ("God, thou art my trust from my youth" [Ps. 71:5, AV]).

Syn. Confidence, Reliance, Dependence, Faith. TRUST implies an assured attitude toward another which may rest on blended evidence of experience and on more subjective grounds such as knowledge, affection, admiration, respect or reverence. [9]

Notice what our first reaction should be when hearing a word from God. The definition of TRUST says we're not to have misgivings about what He has said to us. We are to be completely assured that the Holy Spirit speaks for the Father with complete accuracy. Paul writes in Galatians 3:5 that we are to be free from doubt about the Holy Spirit's work. His works are powerful and miraculous among us. Romans 8:14 and 16 tells us that we are led by the Spirit of God (Holy Spirit) and He is the one who bears witness to our spirits that we are the children of God. Being children of God, adopted into God's family, we are privy to the Father's thoughts, words, and actions. We are also advised in I Corinthians 2 that we have the mind of Christ and can know the thoughts of God.

So, what is to be our first reaction? We are to take the voice of the Spirit at His word. We are to trust Him. Remember, Jesus said He'll (meaning the Holy Spirit) take what is Mine (Jesus') and reveal it to you. In other words, the witness to our spirits will come from the Bible and the voice of the Holy Spirit will confirm it. In this way all misgivings will go, and assurance will come.

Read the account given in Luke 17:3-10. We discover several things pertaining to the gift of Faith in these passages. The apostles were questioning Jesus about the number of times they were required to forgive. Jesus' answer shocked them. He said to forgive a person seven offences if he repented seven times in one day. This was four times more than Jewish law required. In yet another account in Matthew 18:21-22, Jesus admonishes them (his disciples) to forgive seventy times seven. To a Hebrew this was a number too big to comprehend. As the Hebrews understood it, Jesus was telling them to forgive "seventy times seven times seven times seven," ad infinitum. It would be like one hundred trillion times to us. The Jewish faith purported that only three pardons were sufficient. Peter stated that we should forgive seven times. Jesus

emphasized that we should never stop forgiving. When the disciples understood what Jesus was saying, this was their reply, "Lord, increase our faith — that trust and confidence that springs from our belief in God." (AMP)
Let's look at the scripture found in Luke 17:6:

> And the Lord answered, "If you had faith [trust and confidence in God] even as a grain of mustard seed, you could say to this mulberry tree, 'Be pulled up by the roots, and be planted in the sea'; and it would obey you." NAS.

Jesus says if you have faith, trust and confidence in God, even as a grain of mustard seed, your gift of faith will be considered activated enough to move a mulberry tree into a sea. The mustard seed is one of the smallest seeds on earth. The mustard bush, on the other hand, is a very large bush. (Some think this reference was to a tree, but the type of mustard plant indigenous to the area where Jesus lived was a very large and prolific bush.) How can a small seed produce a large bush? It can produce a large bush because the same substance is found in both the seed and the bush. In like manner, that gift of faith which God has placed within you has the potential of being as large as the mustard bush (and just as prolific), but no more than a small amount has to be activated. This is because it is its substance, not its size, that produces trust. This small amount of faith (mustard-seed size) is so effective, so powerful that it could literally pull up a mulberry tree and cast it into the sea. In verse seven, Jesus starts talking about the role of a servant. He is saying to the apostles that if they were allowing the grace of God to operate in them, that which seemed impossible to them in the natural, would be seen as possible in His supernatural. He's saying in verses seven through ten that to forgive seventy times seven is to be expected of us in our positions as servants of the Most High God. We will see the activation of the gift of faith needed to forgive or do anything else as we obey all that He has commanded us to do. He's saying that to trust God is not an option any more than a servant has an option to serve himself before His master. What was Jesus' command? He said that we are to obey the voice of the Spirit, and by so doing, we will fulfill our obligations as servants. He, as Master, is then required to give us our provision, i.e. the ability to forgive seventy times seven through faith or trust in Him. We've heard His will and way and we obey.

God has given you a gift of faith by His grace (unmerited favor). By activating just a small portion of this faith (through trusting Him), you will experience a full life, and you will have supernatural things happening around you. Only a very small amount of this gift needs to be activated in order to trust in, cleave to, rely upon, depend upon and be confident in Him and in what He has said. Whatever He's saying to you today, trust in and adhere to it!

Now let's look at the words "adhere"; "adherence" and "fidelity":

ADHERE — to hold fast or stick by as if by gluing, suction, grasping or fusing — to bind oneself to assurance.[10]

ADHERENCE — steady or faithful attachment.[11]
FIDELITY — to be devoted as a follower or supporter.[12]

Since all your misgivings have been eliminated through TRUST, and you've been assured that you've heard the voice of the Lord, the next step should take place: that of ADHERING. If you hold fast or stick to something, can it be lost? No, it cannot. The Word spoken to you by God will not leave you, but you must stick to or hold fast to it so that *you* don't leave it! I think the definition describing "adhere" as "grasping" is very graphic. Can you see yourself grasping hold of a material object? In the same way, God wants you to see yourself grasping hold of that which He has spoken.

When you've dressed in the morning, you are bound in your clothing. These clothes will stay on until you undress. In the same fashion, God wants you to put on or bind the Word around you. Wear it wherever you go, regardless of anything which seems to contradict what God has said to you.

It's interesting that the word "fidelity" is used to describe *adhering*. Fidelity means remaining true to another. If we fail to adhere to what our Father God is saying to us, we have broken our fidelity to Him. That is a sobering thought!

As we ADHERE to what was spoken, God will supply us with His marvelous Holy Spirit because the active move of God is not dependent upon our fulfilling the Law or a formula. The Holy Spirit will do His work among us as we adhere to His Word and to His power, for we've heard the voice of God in our inner man, and we've seen His will concerning it confirmed in His Word. As the Word and the witness agree, our faith will be ignited and released.

Now let's see what the dictionary has to say about the word "rely":

RELY — to have confidence: have a feeling of security: place faith without reservation: TRUST — used with on, upon, or sometimes in: find support: DEPEND.
Syn. COUNT (on), RECKON (on), BANK (on), TRUST, DEPEND (on): RELY, COUNT, RECKON, and BANK are about equal in force and are often interchangable. RELY may connote an objectivity of judgment: based on previous experience with whatever is in question. [13]

To be confident in another person requires experience that would confirm that person's reliability or dependability. Inherent in the definition of *RELY* is a judgment based upon this experience. If we are to be able to "RELY", this experience will have to prove that the one on whom we are relying cannot fail. Can we, upon reflection, really think that the God of the universe would fail at anything that He willed to do? That would be preposterous! God is still creating, still redeeming, still restoring, still providing, and to suggest any result other than His complete success is ridiculous! I say this in order to put our judgment about His reliability in proper perspective. We are not dealing with another human being in this stage of faith, so we must not draw our conclusions based on our knowledge of man's frailties. After having heard God's specific word for us, we must hold fast to it because God has proven Himself to be reliable, and He will bring His Word to pass.

Since I have personally experienced the reliability of God, let me share from that resource. I am not by natural talents a writer. When God told me to write my first book, *God-Given Territory: A Strategy to Keep It*, I needed to *know* with absolute assurance that this was God. He awakened me three nights in a row and spoke the same thing, "Write for others what I've taught you." Once I was assured that it was God speaking (I trusted the voice), I had to then rely totally on Him if the book were to be written. I had nothing to bring to the endeavor except obedience. The voice of the enemy was constantly attacking with thoughts of unbelief such as: "You know you'd be the last one in your family to write a book. Why don't you hang it up? You're not organized enough to make sense. Even if you get the thing written, it takes money to publish it. Where do you think you could get money like that? Say you get it written and published, who will buy it anyway?" On and on I was besieged with these thoughts, but I kept on obeying, and God kept reassuring me. Through the power of the Holy Spirit and His words, I finished it! Praise God! I remember one Sunday my husband and I were riding up the escalator to the worship service. As I looked down, I saw the vast array of books in the bookstore. The thought came, "Jackie, you may indeed get that book of yours published, but it will never sell." I began to laugh, and my husband asked what was so funny. When I told him about the enemy's latest attempt to sidetrack me, he began to laugh too. Because of Satan's frustrated attack, we *knew* that we *knew* that the book would sell!

At this point we need to take a look at the word "depend":

DEPEND — to trust, rely or place belief or hope often without alternate resource — used with on or upon: to be dependent especially for support —used with in or upon.[14] — *count* (on) and *reckon* (on) imply a taking — to rely upon anything as a source of support or supply. With on or upon; as.... the Christian depends on a divine Savior.[15]

To be supported or assisted is truly liberating. If we were expected by God to walk this walk of faith by ourselves, we would be failures before we began. We can hear the voice of God, bind these words around our necks and write them upon the tablets of our hearts, because we can count on God (Proverbs 3:1-4).

This is what Daniel did. Daniel and his three companions (Shadrach, Meshach, and Abednego) first sought to bind the Word of the Lord around their necks and write them upon their hearts. They sought this from the beginning of their captivity in Babylon. Even after they were selected to be trained for King Nebuchadnezzar's court, they continued their determination to put God first. As a result, they found favor with the commander of the officials and were permitted to continue in their regimentation of diet and prayer. They were able to do this in the midst of a godless court. Why did they do this when the sky was the limit as far as food, drink and pleasures in the king's court were concerned? They knew that to *depend* on anyone other than God could be dangerous! (Daniel 1 & 2)

When we think of Daniel, most of us think of his encounter with the lions, but that was not Daniel's first brush with death at the hands of a king. Daniel, Shadrach, Meshach, and Abednego were being trained for the courts of the king to become wise men. The king would be seeking their advice. If he liked what they said, they lived; if the king didn't like it, they died. It was just that simple!

One day, the king had a dream which perplexed him. Being unable to interpret this dream, he called for the wise men who were present in his court. The King demanded they tell him about the dream and give the interpretation or die. None were able to do so.

When Daniel heard of the king's plan to kill all the wise men, he knew he and his three companions would be called into the king's court to tell about the king's dream and interpret it. Daniel sought the king's permission for Shadrach, Meshach, Abednego and himself to meet together about this dream. Daniel assured the king that he would come before him and bring the interpretation, thereby saving all of them, Babylonians and Israelites alike.

Daniel, Shadrach, Meshach, and Abednego had a full blown prayer meeting! They were in a position of total dependence upon God. The king wouldn't tell anyone the dream, so only through God could the interpretation come forth.

Let's read Daniel 2:19-30:

> Then the mystery was revealed to Daniel in a night vision. Then Daniel blessed the God of heaven;
> Daniel answered and said,
> "Let the name of God be blessed forever and ever,
> For wisdom and power belong to Him.

And it is He who changes the times and the
epochs;
He removes kings and establishes kings;
He gives wisdom to wise men,
And knowledge to men of understanding.
It is He who reveals the profound and hidden
things;
He knows what is in the darkness,
And the light dwells with Him.
To Thee, O God of my fathers, I give thanks and
praise,
For Thou hast given me wisdom and power;
Even now Thou hast made known to me what
we requested of Thee,
For Thou has made known to us the king's
matter."

Therefore, Daniel went to Arioch, whom the king
had appointed to destroy the wise men of Babylon; he
went and spoke to him as follows: "Do not destroy the
wise men of Babylon! Take me into the king's
presence, and I will declare the interpretation to the
king."

Then Arioch hurriedly brought Daniel into the
king's presence and spoke to him as follows: "I have
found a man among the exiles from Judah who can
make the interpretation known to the king!"

The king answered and said to Daniel, whose
name was Belteshazzar, "Are you able to make

known to me the dream which I have seen and its interpretation?"

Daniel answered before the king and said, "As for the mystery about which the king inquired, neither wise men, conjurers, magicians, nor diviners are able to declare it to the king.

"However, there is a God in heaven who reveals mysteries and He has made known to King Nebuchadnezzar what will take place in the latter days. This was your dream and the visions in your mind while on your bed.

"As for you, O king, while on your bed your thoughts turned to what would take place in the future; and He who reveals mysteries has made known to you what will take place.

"But as for me, this mystery has not been revealed to me for any wisdom residing in me more than in any other living man, but for the purpose of making the interpretation known to the king, and that you may understand the thoughts of your mind."

In verse 19, Daniel had a night vision during which he learned all he needed to know in order to tell about the king's dream and give its interpretation. Daniel then declared to God how he always could and did continue to *depend* upon Him. He listed all the reasons he could count on God. Daniel started out by speaking out of his general knowledge of God. He said that all wisdom and power belonged to God, that God was in charge of times and events, that He was well able to establish kings or to remove them. Daniel next declared that God gave wisdom to wise men and knowledge to men and that He took what was profound and hidden and revealed it to us. Notice that all Daniel's previous statements had come from his belief in the law of God which had been bound around his neck. But then he switched to what God had written on the tablets of his heart. Daniel began by speaking of his most recent personal encounter with God's supernatural revelation to his companions and himself. God once again proved Himself dependable, and Daniel rejoiced over the knowledge that they could count on God! Look at all the ways in which Daniel spoke of this:

Verse 23, "To Thee, O God of my fathers, I give thanks and praise,
For Thou hast given *me* wisdom and power;
Even *now* Thou hast made known to *me* what *we* requested of Thee,
For Thou has made known to *us* the king's matter."

Daniel was praising God for the fact that God had spoken to them, answered them personally, and preserved them by this revelation. Danicl's and his companions' lives were certainly contingent upon God's revealing His power and wisdom on their behalf.

Notice how boldly Daniel declared to the king that he and the others laid no claim to the wonder of telling the dream nor to its interpretation. Danicl said this was all caused by the God of heaven!

Daniel was saying to the king, "You are not dealing with me, King Nebuchadnezzar. You are dealing with the

God of the universe. Take heed to what He's doing and saying."

As I stated in the previous chapter, faith expands as we experience more of God's handiwork in our lives. This was certainly true for Daniel.

The same faith that caused Daniel, Meshach, Shadrach, and Abednego to be dependent on God at the beginning of their time in the courts of King Nebuchadnezzar would prepare them to have faith for things to follow.

When Daniel finished telling the king his dream and its interpretation, the king proclaimed the following, in verse 47:

> "Surely, your God is a God of gods and a Lord of kings and revealer of mysteries, since you have been able to reveal this mystery."

Not only did the king acknowledge Daniel's God as God, but he also gave Daniel a position of great authority. It says Daniel made a request of King Nebuchadnezzar, and the king appointed Shadrach, Meshach, and Abednego over the administration of the province of Babylon. I feel God had more in mind to accomplish than simply telling King Nebuchadnezzar the future. God wanted to ensure that His chosen people would be favored, so that they could repent and return to Him. With godly men in positions of power, God's chosen would be able to worship and serve Him.

All four of these young men would have their dependence on God tested as they lived their lives even in the court of the king.

Shadrach, Meshach, and Abednego would have to face

the fiery furnace rather than bow their knees to the image of the king. Their resolve in this matter is best summed up in their statement to King Nebuchadnezzar, "If it be so, our God whom we serve is able to deliver us from the furnace of blazing fire; and He will deliver us out of your hand, O king" (Daniel 3:17).

We see Daniel's dependence on God when King Darius threw him into the den of lions. A document had been signed by the king that no one was to consult God or man but that all were to seek him. This document had been brought to the king by the other commissioners in charge of the kingdom, for the king was considering placing Daniel over all his kingdom, and this enraged them. It was not the king's desire to destroy Daniel, but the document was irrevocable. Here is Daniel's response to this document:

> Now when Daniel knew that the document was signed, he entered his house (now in his roof chamber he had windows open toward Jerusalem); and he continued kneeling on his knees three times a day, praying and giving thanks before God, as he had been doing previously. (Daniel 6:10, NAS)

The exchange between King Darius and Daniel after he was delivered by God from the lions provides another illustration of Daniel's dependence upon God:

> The King spoke and said to Daniel, "Daniel, servant of the living God, has your God, whom you constantly serve, been able to deliver you from the lions?"
>
> Then Daniel spoke to the king, "O king, live forever!

"My God sent His angel and shut the lions' mouths, and they have not harmed me, inasmuch as I was found innocent before Him; and also toward you, O king, I have committed no crime." (Daniel 6:20b-22, NAS)

The impact of Daniel's trust in God was so profound on King Nebuchadnezzar and later, King Darius, that they required all people to acknowledge the God of Daniel. Now, *that* is powerful and it all happened because Daniel and his friends placed their reliance upon God.

In the same way, I knew I would have to depend on God for writing. I knew the book I was to write for God would be written as I relied upon Him. I knew I had to depend upon Him for everything — the words, the wisdom and the resources — or it would not happen.

You might be thinking, "Daniel was Daniel. I'm just an ordinary person. I'm not called by God to live in a king's court." This may be true, but you have the ear of the King of Kings and the Lord of Lords. God used an incident in our son Jeff's life to confirm this lesson to us.

We moved to a new community when Jeff was not quite seven years old. The boys in the new neighborhood had a couple of "pack" leaders. These boys were usually up to no good. Jeff, being the youngest, was the object of their tricks many times. One day one of the leaders asked Jeff to come play dirt hockey. He also promised Jeff that they would not do anything to him. Jeff came to me and asked if he could go. I cautioned him about this boy's past behavior, but Jeff was convinced that this boy was being truthful.

They went out to the vacant lot adjoining our property and began to play. I continued preparing for a visit from a friend of mine. Kris and I were sitting in the kitchen drinking tea when Jeff came running in, gasping for air. He could hardly speak. He was coughing, trying to clear his air passages. I finally was able to piece the story together.

It seemed that this boy and the others had planned to play a trick on Jeff — to tie him to a tree after the game and leave him there. They made good their plan, but in all the struggle, they placed the rope around Jeff's neck and Jeff was being choked!

Jeff, in the natural, was certainly not a match for a half-dozen other boys, so he did what he knew how to do. He began crying out the name of Jesus: "Jesus, Jesus, Jesus help me." All the boys suddenly fell back on the ground, unable to move. The rope loosened and it fell to the ground also. The Lord of Lords had heard Jeff and had delivered him!

Jeff, Kris, and I prayed for the boys and asked God to forgive them. Jeff then went off to bed, exhausted.

Just as the kings of Daniel's day saw the power of God, so the boy who planned this trick also saw God. He came to our home later that afternoon to sincerely ask Jeff for forgiveness. Interestingly, they never tried anything like that again with anyone!

Jeff adhered to the name of Jesus, and God was faithful to act. We knew from this act of God that we could adhere to the name of Jesus, cleave to our God, and never be forsaken! We, like Daniel, have to declare the works of the Lord and of His mighty hand *depending upon Him* to preserve and keep us.

CLEAVE — to adhere firmly and closely or loyally and unwaveringly. Syn. -stick.[14]

A similar word is CLING — to have or continue to have strong emotional or intellectual loyalty or stubborn attachment or belief.[17]

In the scriptures man and woman are instructed to cleave one to the other in their marriage covenant. In the same way, we must cleave to or cling to God to be one with Him. We are to cleave to our "covenant oneness" with our God. This will cause us to cleave to every word He speaks to us.

Mary, the mother of Jesus, gives us such a beautiful example of cleaving to every word God says. Look at her response to the message of the Lord as spoken through Elizabeth in prophecy:

> And blessed is she who believed that there would
> be a fulfillment of what had been spoken to her
> (Mary) by the Lord. (Luke 1:47, NAS)

Cleaving to the message that she would be the mother of a holy child was not, in the natural, an easy message to embrace under Hebrew law. In normal circumstances, Mary would have been found guilty of adultery, since she was betrothed to Joseph, and stoned until dead. How could Mary embrace this and say, "Yes, Lord?" Could it be that Mary remembered the promise to the Hebrew people that the Messiah would be born to a virgin? Could it be that the presence of the Lord was so overpowering that it was more real to her than the Hebrew law? Both God's promise and His presence played a part in her decision, but I think, by the statement which we just read in Luke 1:47, that, more than that, God knew Mary's heart. Mary's heart was ever toward God, and God knew she would cleave to Him and to what He said. Just as importantly, God knew the heart of Joseph, her future husband. God knew that he, too, would cleave to the Lord's words and direction. Both would be mighty servants of God because of their humility. Look what that humility produces: a place for God to enter our world and redeem us! I praise God for their faith's being released by their cleaving to Him.

STAGE III

Resting

REST — "to be free from anxiety or disturbance"
— "to remain confident: TRUST"
— "to place on or against a support" [18]
— "to cause to be firmly fixed: GROUND" [19]

One of the definitions I have found describes rest as "remaining based or founded." I like this definition because I feel it helps us to see the stage of resting in connection with the stages of hearing from God and trusting in Him. To arrive at this new dimension of faith — REST — one must progress through the previous stages.

In other words, having no misgivings that you've heard God's voice and knowing that He can be relied upon become the foundation of our rest.

Notice the definition says, "To remain based or founded." That means that by your progression through the first two stages, a foundation is established in you, which allows you to remain secure and grounded to the point that you are able to rest or lean confidently upon God and upon what He has said. It is like standing in a house and leaning against its walls. You wouldn't lean against the walls if they weren't securely attached to the foundation of the house.

"Rest" also indicates that there is no more struggle in believing what God has spoken. This knowledge becomes an active part of resting by *ignoring* the enemy. It's as if to say, "God, you've confirmed Your will for me by Your Word and Your Spirit. I've walked through the step of trusting You, and now I'm leaning or reclining on all You've worked within me through Your Holy Spirit on this matter." I think you would agree that this is a great place to be.

None of us necessarily likes the struggles we sometimes endure in order to stay in this place of rest, but it's all worth it!

STAGE IV

Yielding

YIELD — to be disposed to submit or comply
— to give or render as fitting, rightfully owed or required

— to surrender or submit (oneself) to another
— to give place or precedence: acknowledge the superiority of someone else
— (syn) DEFER — implies a voluntary yielding or submitting out of respect for reverence for or deference and affection toward another."[20]
— (syn.) RELINQUISH — "to give over possession or control of." [21]

You might ask, "Why is she talking about yielding? It seems to me that if I'm resting in Him for what He said He'd do, that I've fulfilled my part." To this I must say, "Not quite."

Notice in our definition of yielding that it means "to surrender or submit (oneself) to another or to give place to another." It is fitting to give place to another who rightfully owed that position. RELINQUISH is also found as a synonym meaning "to give over possession or control."

Have you ever stumbled upon one of God's truths without realizing it? I stumbled upon the power of yielding without knowing what I was doing or what a powerful effect it would have. It was years after it happened before I even understood the full impact of what I'd done by yielding to God. It had to do with one of the most precious things in our lives, our son

Jeff was our miracle baby. I had had two miscarriages between our second daughter and him. The doctors discovered an imbalance in my hormone levels which was causing these natural abortions. It was determined that we would team our efforts so that when I became pregnant again, I would be given hormone injections as soon as possible to make up for this deficiency. This treatment was religiously followed for the first four and one-half months of my pregnancy with Jeff.

All of us, my husband, our two daughters and I, were thrilled beyond words when this precious gift of God was born. God had answered our prayers.

The first few years of our life with Jeff were filled with delight. We all took pleasure in his pleasant personality. Jeff was a very active child, but none of us were aware that Jeff's level of activity was higher than normal. We assumed that that was the way boys were. We did notice that it was harder for him to adjust to changes than it was for the rest of us.

When Jeff was two and one-half years old, we moved to another state. We had tried to prepare the children for the move, but we could see it was hardest on Jeff. We noticed he'd cry far beyond what would be normal when he had to come home from playing with a friend.

Within the first year after moving, we purchased a beautiful older home which was ideal for us. We settled in to living life in our new surroundings.

Things were going well with Rog's work: the girls were in an excellent school, and Jeff and I were happily living our lives on the homefront. This life was to continue, uninterrupted, for about a year.

Rog's research had been so successful that he was to take the research team's precious sample to Stanford University to put through a special analytical machine to help them characterize the hormone factor they had extracted. The timing was such that Rog flew to California the Friday before the fourth of July and was scheduled to be gone until the following week.

By now, the children had adjusted to the fact that Rog's work required him to leave us for a week or two at a time. We took him to the airport and returned home. It was just another part of our routine as far as I was concerned. The girls went about occupying themselves with play, and I really didn't pay much attention to Jeff's activities.

We had supper, and I put them to bed. It was then that I realized Jeff was asking for his Daddy. He seemed to be very persistent. I tried to explain to Jeff that Daddy was on a plane, and that we couldn't reach him by phone, reasoning with him that we could call him in the morning. This didn't seem to pacify Jeff at all! Throughout the night he was in our bedroom, pleading with me to have his Daddy come home and insisting that he wanted him to come right away. I didn't know what to do. We were regular churchgoers, and we were involved in church activities, but I never thought to pray for God's help. By morning I was exhausted! I noticed over the course of that sleepless night that Jeff had developed a slight fever and a runny nose. I thought to myself, "Oh! This is why Jeff is so hard to handle."

I came down the stairs still in my nightclothes, planning to fix the kids breakfast and then to ask Lynn and Lori to watch Jeff for me so I could get a little rest.

As I was preparing breakfast, I heard Jeff start to repeat his request, "I want my Daddy. I want him home with me."

Now he was walking around in circles, repeating it again and again. I turned to assure him that Daddy would talk with him by phone that morning and then I finished putting the children's breakfast on the table. I went back up the stairs to get some rest and left the girls in charge of watching Jeff. I was only in bed a very short while when I heard Lynn screaming. I came running down the stairs to see Jeff shaking violently. I'd never seen a seizure before in my life, but instantly I knew what was happening. I quickly grabbed Jeff up in my arms, put a popsicle stick between his teeth and told the girls to follow me. Between the three of us, we kept him from harming himself. Just as suddenly as the seizure had begun, it stopped. Jeff lay on our bed, unconscious.

I asked the girls to keep the stick readied, and I quickly dressed and called our neighbor. I asked her to hold Jeff and to do whatever was necessary if another seizure should occur while I was driving him to the emergency room at the children's hospital in our community.

For what seemed to be an eternity, the girls, our neighbor and I waited to talk with the doctors. During this time, however, I was able to gather my thoughts, and I called one of my husband's associates (who was a medical doctor) and asked if he would call Rog for me and then come over to be with us. I was so grateful to him. He dropped everything and was by our side within minutes of my call.

Finally the doctors came in with their preliminary report. They had ruled out hemorrhaging caused by a broken blood vessel. From the conversation they were having with my husband's associate, I gathered they had thought that was what they were dealing with and they had waited, hoping that was not the case. They knew that if that were the case, we'd lose Jeff. After an E.E.G., they were satisfied that they were not looking at hemorrhaging of the brain; rather, a part of Jeff's brain had suffered brain damage. The damage had caused the seizure.

When they had completed all their tests, their initial findings were confirmed. Now they would have to determine what the effect of this damage would be, and what would be the appropriate treatment.

They let us see Jeff. As I held our little four-year-old, I was so grateful that he was still with us. I explained to him that he'd have to stay, but that I'd come right back as soon as I had taken the girls home. In his own exhaustion, Jeff went into a sound sleep.

When I arrived home, the phone was ringing. It was Rog. He had tried desperately to find a flight home, but there were no flights available. The fourth of July was a busy time. I would be on my own with the kids and Jeff's situation until Monday.

I left the girls with a precious neighbor and returned to the hospital.

Jeff was a real trooper throughout all the tests. I was so grateful to our neighbors for watching the girls so that I could be with Jeff every step of the way.

For the next two days, I ran between the hospital and home, trying to alleviate any fears the girls or Jeff might have had. I count it a blessing that I was not fully aware of all the possible medical consequences which existed.

The tests were completed, and the doctors were now comfortable with letting Jeff go home with us. As Rog and I walked into the doctor's office on Monday, we weren't sure what to expect. We didn't know what effect the brain damage would have on Jeff.

We were blessed in that Jeff's hospital had one of the leading children's neurological centers in the United States. Jeff's doctor began by explaining the location of the brain damage, what he and his associates recommended medically, and what they would expect to happen, based on their recommended treatment. He also told us the following things:

1. Jeff would continue to have seizures even though, they felt, the damage would heal. The medication would control the seizures, to an extent. The scar tissue would always remain, and this scar tissue would trigger seizures.

2. Jeff's hyperactivity was directly connected to the brain damage.

3. Jeff would require two forms of medicine. One, to suppress the seizures, would have to be taken for life. The other, to control the hyperactivity, he would have to take until he grew out of it (if he was going to), which they could not guarantee.

4. The medications had side effects. One of them could have the side effect of developing aplastic anemia. This is an irreversible blood disorder. The doctor did assure us

that the percentage of people developing this side effect on this medication was very small.

Rog and I walked out of the doctor's office believing that his recommendation and evaluations were right. I think we were in a state of numbness though, trying to view logically what had to be done medically and mixing that with the fact that our son's life and ours could be under the shadow of seizures and side-effects.

Rog returned to work, and I went on home and retrieved the children from a neighbor.

It was close to lunchtime when I arrived home, so I fed the children and took Jeff to his room for his nap. I found it hard to believe that there was anything wrong with this precious miracle baby of ours.

The girls headed for the neighborhood pool, and I was left with my thoughts. Our dog, Jeff's best buddy, was making it known that he wanted out. I thought, "I'll just step out in the yard with him. I need to find a place of quietness."

The sun was brilliant, and the foliage was such a vivid green that I found it breathtaking. I heard myself saying, "Lord, thank You for these surroundings. You know, God, Jeff is a miracle baby. You gave him to us. God, if Jeff develops these side effects the doctor told us about, and he dies, I will thank You for every day You gave him to us. He's really Yours anyway, and if we have him a month, a year or for many years, we will always thank You for the treasure of our time with him. He is still our miracle from You."

I suddenly experienced a flooding of peace over my entire being. Somehow I knew that that peace would never leave me. I knew that as I took Jeff for his monthly blood tests that peace would sustain us both.

For the next two and one-half years, Jeff and I would make our monthly trip to have his blood tested. Each time this beautiful peace would rest upon us. Our lives seemed to return to normal. For reasons which the doctors could not explain, Jeff did not experience any more seizures. This puzzled the doctors because of the type of seizure Jeff had had. It had been a grand mal and that type usually indicates forthcoming recurrences.

Rog came home from work one day and announced that his whole research team had been offered positions and space in a well-established research institute in California. This was a golden opportunity for the team as a whole, so they decided to move to this new lab.

Since we would be moving shortly, it was necessary for us to update Jeff's medical history in preparation for the neurologist in our new community. All the tests that had been performed on Jeff when he first experienced the seizure were once again performed. We made an appointment with our doctor to hear the evaluation and to pick up the records to take with us.

As Rog and I walked into his office, he was shaking his head as he was poring over a medical record. It turned out to be Jeff's medical record. He said, "I don't understand how this is possible, but we can't find any vestige of scar tissue. It's as if Jeff had never had brain damage." He showed us the first results and the X-rays showing the location of the damage. Then he showed us the most recent series. We, too, were bewildered by this, but thoroughly delighted! Jeff could stop taking the medicine, and he would not have to live under the threat of the possible side effects.

It was a full year after we had moved to California before we knew what had happened to Jeff.

By then, we had renewed our commitment to Jesus Christ and had experienced the release of the Holy Spirit's power in our lives. During that year, we learned of the healing power of God. Without our knowledge of His healing power, God had healed Jeff. He was our miracle! I had turned Jeff over to God the Father, for His care. Since God was to care for him, He did!

We took that principle of yielding and used it for the rearing of Jeff and the girls. This has been the greatest thing in our lives: to be able to give them back to the Father God for His care. Praise God forevermore!

At one time we didn't know what we were doing, but now we do. Now we see that the peace we experienced throughout all of this was God's promise to us that all was well. Now we know we can have assurance through the peace of God and the voice of the Holy Spirit.

This is not a new truth we are addressing, for throughout the scriptures we see the principle of yielding in operation. By faith, Abraham yielded to God and relinquished Issac. Paul and Silas yielded to God's powerful presence in prison and were set free. Jesus yielded to the will of His Father and died, even though He was promised that He would become King of Kings and Lord of Lords. We can experience peace, comfort, power and freedom just like our forefathers enjoyed when we turn everything over to God. We, too, can place all things concerning us into His hands for His mighty touch (Genesis 22, Acts 16:25-34, Matthew 26).

I want to encourage you to let the Holy Spirit take you through the different stages of faith in your relationship with the Father. Take the promise (your personal word from God) which God has given to you. Cling to it, trust in it and adhere to it, and then lay it at the feet of God. By so doing, you'll be saying, "Here, Father, this is Yours. You gave it to me; now I submit it to You so You can bring this promise to pass in Your way and Your time. I leave it entirely up to You. I lay no claim to having any power to bring it into manifestation. May Your way and will be proclaimed and may Your Name be glorified."

PART III

Jesus — An Example of Perfect Faith

As we study the Gospels, we know that much took place in Jesus' life between His water baptism and the cross. This is what we need to investigate in order to see faith in operation. If we can look to Jesus for the way (He said He is the Way) of operation in faith, we'll be able to take what we know and apply it. We'll find an inner strength, the same strength that caused Jesus to fulfill God's will and that caused Jesus to receive what the Father promised.

In Genesis 3:14-15, God promised to remove the headship or rule of Satan over mankind, and that this rule would be transferred to Jesus ("the seed of the woman"). This depended on Jesus yielding to the will of the Father.

God devised a solution for our captivity and *spoke this plan to Jesus* (STAGE I) Stage one had been accomplished.

Let's read Mark 1:9-11:

And it came about in those days that Jesus came from Nazareth in Galilee, and was baptized by John in the Jordan, and immediately coming up out of the water, He saw the heavens opening, and the Spirit like a dove descending upon Him; and a voice came out of the heavens: "Thou art My beloved Son, in Thee I am well-pleased."

Jesus came to the river Jordan to carry out an act of obedience to the Father and in so doing demonstrated He had *no misgivings* (STAGE II) about what He was to do and believe. He submitted His flesh to the faith-progression the Father had selected. From the Father's statement we know that this act of obedience was pleasing to the Father. Jesus had had *a specific word from God* and *He had trusted and relied upon God* to fulfill that word.

Jesus also consented to follow the path selected for Him by the Father. Immediately after the Father's recognition of Jesus' sonship and His declaration of pleasure with Jesus' obedience, Jesus was impelled by the Holy Spirit to go into the wilderness, where, for forty days, Satan tried to dislodge Jesus' faith in His Father. Every one of Jesus' replies illustrated His position of *rest or leaning upon* the spoken word of God. In other words, Jesus was walking in the THIRD STAGE of faith, "resting."

In Matthew 26 we have the first-hand account of Jesus walking in the final stage of faith. He came to Gethsemane from a place of preparation.

Let's read Matthew 26:36-44:

> Then Jesus came with them to a place called Gethsemane, and said to His disciples, "Sit here while I go over there and pray." And He took with Him, Peter and the two sons of Zebedee, and began to be grieved and distressed. Then He said to them, "My soul is deeply grieved, to the point of death; remain here and keep watch with Me." And He went a little beyond them, and fell on His face and prayed, saying,

"My Father, if it is possible, let this cup pass from Me; yet not as I will, but as Thou wilt." And He came to the disciples and found them sleeping, and said to Peter, "So, you men could not keep watch with Me for one hour? Keep watching and praying, that you may not enter into temptation; the spirit is willing, but the flesh is weak." He went away again a second time and prayed, saying, "My Father, if this cannot pass away unless I drink it, Thy will be done." And He came back and found them sleeping, for their eyes were heavy. And He left them again, and went away and prayed a third time, saying the same thing once more.

As we read the account of Jesus' return to pray for the third time in order to walk through His own personal struggle to *yield* (STAGE IV) Himself wholly to the Father's will, we come face to face with the true meaning of yielding. Jesus surrendered all He had — Himself.

This final operation of Jesus' faith came from a season of preparation which enabled Him to surrender all to His Father. This stage would produce the greatest benefit to mankind ever and the consequences of this act of faith are continuing today. Every time a new person is brought into the kingdom, Jesus' act of faith two thousand years ago is further manifested!

Sometimes, I think, we as Christians take for granted Jesus' sacrifice. God forbid, but it becomes commonplace. If we go back and look at the anguish Jesus suffered in making that decision to yield to the Father's will, we'll see just how rough it was to say "yes."

Jesus had never known separation from the presence of the Father, even while on earth. He had never personally experienced sin and its destructiveness. He was asked to take all the sins of mankind unto Himself, thereby causing a separation from His Father. Jesus was being asked to trust the Father with His eternal life as well. He would be totally dependent upon God to deliver Him. Have you ever considered the fact that once Jesus said "yes," He'd have to rely upon the Father and the Holy Spirit to bring Him back from His mission to Hell? This is also the ultimate in yielding, that Jesus gave himself and the situation totally to God's control, producing the ultimate: total victory over Satan and His demons. In the same way, we, as sons of God, can experience the victory of God's completed will for us in our lives if we allow Him to take us through these four stages of faith.

FAITH: LIVING EACH STEP IN THE PRESENT

Once I was teaching on the operation of our faith, and a dear saint asked me this question: "If we walked through these four stages once, would that complete the operation of our faith for all that God would later speak to us?" I had to say no.

Jesus said at one point in His ministry that He did only what was assigned to Him by the Father. By this statement, Jesus was telling us that He continually walked through these stages of faith and that this pleased His Father.

What was true for Jesus is true for us. Each time God speaks something new to us, these stages in the operation of our faith must be walked through again. That may mean that in the midst of God's communicating several promises or things for you to do, you may find yourself in different stages of faith for the various things He's spoken to you. While one thing is readied for manifestation, there is another promise waiting for the cycle to be completed. Keep in mind Who it is that is bringing all of these things to pass.

It is marvelous to see the way the Holy Spirit nourishes us, strengthens us, empowers us, and lovingly brings us through each stage of the operation of faith for a given promise or mission.

When we reflect upon the way He worked to bring forth the manifestation of things He has promised in the past, we will always marvel at His handiwork. It will cause us to press on, excited about His handiwork in our future.

Footnotes

- 1 (page 2) — Scripture quotations are from the Amplified New Testament, Lockman Foundation 1954, 1958.
- 2 (page 35) — Books of Exodus, Joshua, Ruth and Nehemiah.
- 3 (page 38) — Song: "What a Friend," written by Joseph Scrives and Charles C. Converse. Under public domain.
- 4 (page 38) — I Samuel 19:9-24
- 5 (page 38) — Psalm 60:11-12
- 6 (page 7) — Psalm 86:14-17
- 7 (page 62) — Moody Press. *The Wycliffe Commentary*, edited by Charles F. Pfeiffer, Old Testament; and Everett F. Harrison, New Testament. Copyright by Moody Bible Institute 1962.
- 8 (page 68) — If you have not experienced the release of the Holy Spirit, you many want to order my tape entitled, "Releasing the Holy Spirit in You." An order form may be found in the back of this book.
- 9 (page 71) — "By permission. From *Webster's Third New International Dictionary*, 1986 by Merriam-Webster Inc., publisher of the Merriam-Webster Dictionaries." Page 2456.

- 10 (page 76) — "By permission. From *Webster's Ninth New Collegiate Dictionary*, 1986 by Merriam-Webster Inc., publisher of the Merriam-Webster Dictionaries." Page 56.
- 11 (page 76) — "By permission. From *Webster's Third New International Dictionary*, 1986 by Merriam-Webster Inc., publisher of the Merriam-Webster Dictionaries." Page 1531.
- 12 (page 76) — 1985 by Houghton Mifflin Company. Reprinted by permission from the *American Heritage Dictionary, Second College Edition*. Page 79.
- 13 (page 77) — "By permission. From *Webster's Third New International Dictionary*, 1986 by Merriam-Webster Inc., publisher of the Merriam-Webster Dictionaries." Page 1919.
- 14 (page 79) — "By permission. From *Webster's Third New International Dictionary*, 1986 by Merriam-Webster Inc., publisher of the Merriam-Webster Dictionaries." Page 604.
- 15 (page 79) — Reprinted from *Funk and Wagnall's New Standard Dictionary of English Language* 1983 by permission of J.G. Ferguson Publishing Company, Chicago, Illinois. Page 683.
- 16 (page 88) — "By permission. From *Webster's Ninth New Collegiate Dictionary*, 1986 by Merriam-Webster Inc., publisher of Merriam-Webster Dictionaries." Page 247.

- 17 (page 88) — "By permission. From *Webster's Third New International Dictionary*, 1986 by Merriam-Webster Inc., publisher of the Merriam-Webster Dictionaries." Page 423.
- 18 (page 89) — "By permission. From *Webster's Ninth New Collegiate Dictionary*, 1986 by Merriam-Webster Inc., publisher of Merriam-Webster Dictionaries." Page 1005.
- 19 (page 89) — "By permission. From *Webster's Third New International Dictionary*, 1986 by Merriam-Webster Inc., publisher of the Merriam-Webster Dictionaries." Page 1936
- 20 (page 90) — "By permission. From *Webster's Ninth New Collegiate Dictionary*, 1986 by Merriam-Webster Inc., publisher of Merriam-Webster Dictionaries." Page 1365.
- 21 (page 90) — "By permission. From *Webster's Ninth New Collegiate Dictionary*, 1986 by Merriam-Webster Inc., publisher of Merriam-Webster Dictionaries." Page 995.

Bibliography

Moody Press. *The Wycliffe Commentary* edited by Charles F. Pfeiffer, Old Testament and Everett F. Harrison, New Testament, © copyright by Moody Bible Institute, Chicago, IL 60645, 1962.

By permission. From *Webster's Third New International Dictionary* © 1986 by Merriam-Webster Inc., publisher of the Merriam-Webster Dictionaries, Springfield, MA 01101.

By permission. From *Webster's Ninth New Dictionary* © 1986 by Merriam-Webster Inc., publishers of the Merriam-Webster Dictionaries, Springfield, MA 01101.

Reprinted by permission. From the *American Heritage Dictionary, Secondary College Edition* © 1985 by Houghton Mifflin Company, Boston, MA 02108

Reprinted from *Funk and Wagnall's New Standard Dictionary of English Language,* © 1983 by permission of J.G. Ferguson Publishing Company, Chicago, IL.

By permission. Taken from the *Dicken's New Analytical Bible & Dictionary of the Bible.* World Bible Publishers, Inc. © 1973 City Iowa Falls, Iowa 50126.

Scriptures Quotations are from the *New American Standard Bible,* © The Lockman Foundation 1960, 1962, 1963, 1971, 1972, 1973, 1975, 1977. Note: All scripture quotations unless otherwise indicated are from the *New American Standard Bible* by the Lockman Foundation. La Habra, CA 90631.

"The book, "God Given Territory: A Strategy to Keep It!," will help believers to know their rights and how to stand upon them. It states the Word of God simply, yet authoritatively. You can count on it to build your faith."

BILLY JOE DAUGHERTY, Pastor
Victory Christian Center
Tulsa, Oklahoma

Our New Album is Now Available

Let Your Glory Come!

God's desire is for us to come into His presence. Understanding the glory of God will usher us into His presence, His will, and cause abundant joy to be ours.

20% Off   Sale Price $9.60

Jackie Burgus Ministries Catalog

Single Teaching Tapes:

HDO01   Having Done All to Stand .... $ 4.00
(How to stand in the Battle.)

TS01   Who Controls Time and Space?................ $ 4.00
(Learn how we're not bound by either.)

RH001   Releasing the Holy Spirit in You .... $ 4.00
(Learn how to experience
the fullest God wants for You.)

CV01   Catch the Vision God Has for You .... $ 4.00

WK01   Word of Knowledge .... $ 4.00
(How it works and how to recognize it.)

XFY001   Til Christ be Formed in You .... $ 4.00
(A look at what causes Godly lives.)

HYG02   His Yoke Gives Rest.......................... $ 4.00
(Feel tired and weary? — Jesus is the answer.)

GIV001   And They in Turn Gave .... $ 4.00
(Jesus taught the disciples how
to experience God's multiple blessings.)

REV01   Is Revival In You? .... $ 4.00
(Revival must first come to the Saints.)

WME001   Watchman on the Wall .... $ 4.00
(There is a need for strategic prayer
to build the kingdom of God.)

Single Teaching Tapes:

HEZ001 Hezekiah: His Plan was No Plan .... $ 4.00
Except to Do God's Will

GG01 God's Glory Brings Belief .... $ 4.00

GG02 God's Glory: Who Proclaims It? .... $ 4.00

WOJ02 The Wonder of Jesus .... $ 4.00

IHP001 In His Presence .... $ 4.00
(Come into God's throne room.)

Special Music Tape:

FHT01 From Him: To You .... $ 4.00
(Jackie, accompanied by her autoharp, sings the songs
God has given her.)

Books:

WHT150 God-Given Territory: .... $ 2.95
A Strategy to Keep It!

WGT150 Where Are We in God's Timetable? .... $ 1.50
(What's on the heart of the Father?)

Tape Albums:

HT001-06 God-Given Territory: $28.00
     A Strategy to Keep It! (6 tapes)

INT01-06 Intercession $28.00
     Foundations of Intercession (6 tapes)

GT01-04 Where Are We In $20.00
     God's Timetable? (4 tapes)

WWW01-04 Wisdom: What It Is and $20.00
     How do We Get It? (4 tapes)

FG001-04 Faith: Given and Activated $20.00
     A Balanced Look at Faith (4 tapes)

NCL01-03 Can This Be Normal for Christians? $16.00
     Are we to expect persecution? (3 tapes)

	Please send	Amt encl
Catalog Number:	_____________	$ _________
Catalog Number:	_____________	$ _________
Send check to:	Total:	$ _________

Jackie Burgus Ministeries

P.O. Box 701822
Tulsa, Oklahoma 74170

Add 7% tax for OK residents
Add $1.00 for shipping and handling

Notes

Notes

Notes

Notes

Notes